Foreword

The Heysham peninsula is one of those hidden corners of England, full of interest but little-known outside its immediate locality. Like all peninsulas, it is a place on the edge, balanced between land and water. Wind, sea and wide skies are omnipresent and the inland skyline of Lancaster with the backdrop of the Bowland fells seems further away than the few miles which, in reality, separate the 'mainland' and peninsular sides of the Lune estuary.

This collection of vivid vignettes will be welcomed by visitors and residents alike. In it are described the natural heritage of the peninsula, as well as its varied past, brought alive by nuggets of local history and reminiscences of former times. Probably the best known aspects of Heysham's heritage are St Patrick's chapel and St Peter's church, both evocative legacies from the medieval past, and Sambo's Grave at Sunderland Point, an equally evocative reminder of the days when the Lune was part of the unholy web of the slave trade. But other, forgotten shadows of the past are also recaptured here: the 'wild west' shanty towns of Klondyke and Dawson City, housing the navvies who built Heysham harbour a century ago; and the entertainers and amusements on Heysham Head.

There is nostalgia here, of course, and it will call forth further memories from the older generation who remember the area in the first half half the twentieth century; but for visitors and newer residents I hope that this book will add to their enjoyment when exploring this unique corner of Lancashire.

Angus Winchester
Lancaster University

The Heysham Peninsula

Reprinted from 1st Edition Ordnance Survey Sheet No. 15. 1865 No. XC1

The Heysham Peninsula

The area covered in this account is shaped like an inverted triangle with a tail. Sunderland Point is the 'tail', a peninsula of its own. Overton is a short way up the east side of the triangle, a little inland from the River Lune, whilst Heysham is up the west side on Morecambe Bay. This, with Middleton, is the area we have called the Heysham Peninsula.

*The book is dedicated to the memory of
John Cragg Procter (1930 - 1997),
whose enthusiasm and resourcefulness contributed greatly to
the reawakening of interest in Heysham's history.*

**Heritage
HEYSH
Association
M**

Mesolithic Scraper

2000

Supported by
Millennium Awards for All

The Heysham Peninsula, ed. Eileen Dent
Published © by Heysham Heritage Association (HHA)
Secretary: Barbara Verhoef, 80 Twemlow Parade, Heysham LA3 2AL
The Editor and contributors have generously donated all copyright in this edition to HHA.
The copyright of all the images remains with the originators.

HHA was founded in 1990 and has over 100 members.
It is a voluntary society devoted to the heritage of Heysham.
All proceeds from the sale of this book will go to HHA funds for conservation of the heritage of Heysham, in particular the Heritage Centre. Donations towards the cost of publication were received from Brian Hugo, and from friends of John C Procter in his memory.
HHA works in partnership with
the Heritage Trust for the North West, Registered Charity No. 508300

All rights reserved
No part of this publication may be reproduced, stored in a retrieval system, or transmitted in any form or by any means, mechanical, electronic, photocopying, recording, or otherwise, without the prior permission of Heysham Heritage Association.

ISBN 0 9530303 2 6

Heysham Peninsula
Contents

	Foreword	i
	Acknowledgements	vi
1.	Geology (and some history)	1
2.	Natural Heritage	5
3.	St Patrick's Chapel	13
4.	St Peter's Church	16
5.	They came to Heysham	20
6.	Heysham Harbour	25
7.	Living and Making a Living	34
8.	A Gardener's Diary	39
9.	Pastimes and Entertainments	42
10.	Heysham Head	43
11.	Some Heysham Buildings	47
12.	History beneath my feet	51
13.	Education	53
14.	Storms	61
15.	Heysham Village Institute	63
16.	Overton	66
17.	Middleton	69
18.	Sunderland Point	70
	Bibliography	72
	Index	73

Heysham Peninsula
Acknowledgements

In editing this book I have received a great deal of help. There have been articles submitted, and I have used the writings of historians, and a diarist, from the past. Many of the pictures have been loaned and copied. I have interviewed inhabitants and those who have lived in the area. Many people have offered 'snippets' which have confirmed information received. I have chatted to local people about Heysham, Overton and Middleton. I would like to register my thanks for the contributions of those named, some posthumously, and as an off-comer apologise for my own short-comings.

Edgar Baxter	Rod Hargreaves	Irene Morris
Edward Baxter	Kevin Helm	Chris Nightingale
Arthur Casson	Mary Hill	Peter Preston
Colin Coomber	David Hodgson	Doreen Read
Brenda Coomber	F Whewell Hogarth	John Read
Jean Curwen	John Holding	Tony Ross
Stanley Curwen	Margaret Hunt	Everard Royds
Curwen Sisters: Amy, Daisy	Jim Hutchinson	Freda Smalley
Maud Sinkinson	Laytham Sisters	Fraser Smalley
Bill Dean	Margaret Robson	Barbara Verhoef
Margaret Dean	Ruth Seary	Maureen Walker
Frank Dodgson	Alice Shearing	Ben Walker
Jean Exton	Margaret Manning	Jim Whittaker
Norman Gibson	David Milnes	
Katherine Gregson	John Morris	

Additional thanks to John Holding who did the typesetting and image processing (using Impression Publisher and Imagemaster on a RiscPC), to Rod Hargreaves for some of the illustrations, and to Jean Exton for proof-reading. To Lynn Wilman and the Morecambe Reference Library Staff who helped with their usual patience. To Andrew White and Nigel Dalziel, Curators of the Lancaster City and Maritime Museums, who very kindly allowed me to browse through their collection of pictures, some of which are printed here, with permission (pages 3, 25, 26, 30, 33). To Jennifer Rennie, Gallery Manager at Haworth Art Gallery, Accrington, for permission to include a monochrome image of *Heysham in Winter* by William Woodhouse (page 24).

The outer cover features the painting *A Lancashire Village : 1908* by William Page Atkinson Wells (1872-1923) and is reproduced with the permission of Ian O'Riordan, Keeper of Fine Art Collections at the City Art Centre, Edinburgh. It depicts Second Terrace at Sunderland Point. The cover design is by Rod Hargreaves.

Heysham Peninsula
1. *Geology* (and some History!)

Heysham itself is a piece of land on the Morecambe Bay side of the peninsula. The original parish boundary stretched from the Battery to what is now the harbour.

At its southern extremity is a point formed of New Red Sandstone Rocks and was once called 'Red Nab', largely gone now because of the Power Station and the Harbour. Before the harbour there was a cliff of boulder clay rather less than 100 ft high and two rocky points, Far Naze and Near Naze, now incorporated into the harbour complex. Most of the inner part of Morecambe Bay ebbs dry at the low water of spring tides.

North of the harbour is Half Moon Bay, then Heysham Head and Throbshaw Point, these forming a promontory about 130 ft in height of millstone grit and sandstone. A little further north a cliff of boulder clay has now been formed into the Sunshine Slopes of Cross Cop. These cliffs of boulder clay have been much eroded during the last hundred years. Boulders both large and small on the beach, and out on the skears, are what is left after the red marl has been

Ordnance Survey Map (1915) of Heysham and the Harbour after construction.

Geology/History

washed away. One or two interesting boulders have been left on the Slopes.

The boulder clay represents ridges of detritus or moraines left by glaciers during the Ice Age. Hence the boulders are round, having been ground, the ridges themselves showing the direction of the glacier movement, whilst the boulders are limestone, bluestone, greenstone and granite, the last having travelled from Shap.

On the very top of these ridges is seen the curious phenomenon of springs of water breaking out. These are not the usual surface water, but have come from deep sources owing to the terrific strain on the underlying strata.

The New Red Sandstone, hardening as it does with time and exposure, makes good building-stone.

Flint is not found in this district and so the axes and hammers of the Stone Age were made of bluestone.

During the 1992 archaeological dig flint tools were found. The archaeologists explained this as an import from northern France where flints of this kind are found in abundance. At the time - 12,000 years ago - such materials were brought by traders sailing up the Irish Sea and into Morecambe Bay. The local people would work on them and turn them into tools. Artefacts of a similar kind have been found in various places in Morecambe Bay.

Heysham Lake represents a prehistoric valley, now submerged. It extends from Heysham Skears, past the harbour, between Middleton Sands and Clark's Wharf down into the Lune Deeps. Peat, bog oak and the horns of prehistoric red deer are sometimes dredged up by fishermen, especially just south of the harbour.

On Heysham Moss are the remnants of a morass which extended along the right bank of the Lune from Skerton to Overton. It was impassable to strangers up to recent times. Peat is still out there. As fuel it is little used, but it possesses the remarkable property when burnt of having a wave-length very different from that of a gas or electric fire, so that the heat penetrates right through the human body, warming the back as well as the front (*Arthur Casson[1] can find no evidence to prove this*).

Some of the burial places were called Long Barrows. In Heysham, as opposed to other similar relics in various parts of the country, these Long Barrows may have been formed by the action of glaciers during the Ice Age, coming up against an outcrop of rock, thus forming a piled up mound of detritus. In the case of other glacial ridges in the district, a section reveals stones of different types embedded in a matrix of red marl, all the stones being rounded by the grinding of the moving glacier. Moreover, in these ridges are cavities and pits where the marl has been easily dug out for agricultural uses. In the Heysham Barrows are large areas formed of packed stones of comparatively soft material (grit) the edges of which are still sharp and the chinks between not filled up with clay. Rabbits have never used the Barrows as warrens, although all other glacial ridges have been freely used as such.

The Barrows have not been excavated. When an archaeological dig took place on a flat piece of land below St Patrick's Chapel in 1992, turning up lots of evidence of previous occupation, it was decided to leave the mounds for future generations to investigate.

Early inhabitants

Whilst there is no doubt that people lived in the area 12,000 years ago - the archaeological finds leave no doubt of that - what we don't know is whether the land was in continuous occupation. Certainly lifestyles changed. From hunter gatherers, people became farmers and cultivated the land.

The earliest known settlers were the Celts, and Arthur Casson[2] (*in a document undated, but probably about 30 years old*) tells us that:

> ... in Heysham they were from a tribe called Segantii of the race known as Brigantes. They worshipped the Sun, their priests were Druids and their doctrines included Transmigration of Souls.

The Celts were wonderful weavers of osiers. They could make a basket to hold in a prisoner. The fishing baulks on the skears would be woven originally by the Celts in osiers, but hazel is used mainly today. Even today a well-kept baulk is the most ingenious device ever invented for providing a constant supply of fresh fish, whatever the weather. It is hard trying work, twice daily. The names came later: 'baulk' is Anglo-Saxon and 'skear' is Norse. Casson writes:

> Other relics of the Celts in Heysham are the home made baskets for fish and mussels called 'teanels'. Still made there and used regularly, and also a bottle-shaped eel trap made of woven osiers.

Fish Baulks (c.1890) : John Walker

Geology/History

It was during this period that Christianity was brought to Heysham and other places in the North West by missionaries from Ireland.

Angles

Although the next age is referred to as the Anglo-Saxon Age, Saxons did not come to Heysham. The Angles did.
This again from Casson's History:

> Angles from the south of Jutland raided the NE coast, and during ... 50 years had burned and blasted their way right through the country and by AD 600 under Athelfrith had over-run the district. Probably the Celts welcomed the Angles in order to keep away the Picts, preferring the lesser evil. The fact remains that Heysham district now became Anglian whilst the few remaining Celts lived in harmony with them.

Towards the end of the 9th century the Danes came to Heysham. They were also settlers, and may have been escaping religious persecution in the Isle of Man. There may have only been one family, but it is believed that the hogback stone, now in Heysham Church, was a memorial to an honoured chief.

Normans

Although William the Conqueror came in 1066 he did not bother Heysham much. At the time of the Battle of Hastings, Heysham belonged to Tostig, then said to be living at Halton. His brother Harold was killed at the Battle of Hastings. Heysham is mentioned in the Domesday book, and various spellings have been used: Hessayne, Hessam, but for at least the last 150 years it has been pronounced Hee-sham. Since the time of the Conqueror the manor has passed through many hands, the Lord of the Manor often appropriating Heysham as a surname.

> In 1208 a robber-chief called 'Little Dick' attacked the Manor House at Heysham and was killed. He was Richard Dorme from Latham who had served in the Crusades against Saladin. The Vicar of Heysham, Dom Roberto, from St Mary's Priory, Lancaster, took charge of the body and had a stone coffin hewn out of the rock.

References
1. Arthur Casson : *History of Heysham* : unpublished, c.1965
2. Arthur Casson : *op.cit.*

Heysham Peninsula
2. *Natural Heritage*

Local Habitats

The peninsula is a mixture of rural and suburban areas, of industrial sites, and of river estuary and coastline.

The suburban areas are principally to the west along the coast, both north and south of Heysham village extending inland to the railway line, and around the old villages of Overton and Middleton. The identity of Heysham village is still enhanced by greenfield coast to the north and to the west; the National Trust now owns the Barrows field with the historic site of St Patrick's Chapel, together with a strip of wild land above the cliffs towards Half Moon Bay. The Trust has also declared an interest in purchasing the agricultural land to the north of the village. The settlement at Overton is as old as that at Heysham and the village there has retained its character.

The rural areas are principally pasture and silage with a small amount of arable land for crops. This area is easily seen from the new bypass road from Lancaster to the Harbour. To the east is some higher land rising to 30m above Colloway Marsh on the Lune estuary, but the central and northern area is low lying and extensively drained by a complex network of ditches. In severe weather this area was subject to flood on high spring tides. A substantial part of the western side was once mossland, but the extensive drainage has reduced it to a small fragment of raised bog, a very rare habitat in Lancashire, just to the east of the railway line.

There is a little woodland around Heysham and Overton villages and a larger amount adjacent to the mossland; some screen planting was done at Middleton to 'hide' the industrial sites and this has been repeated more recently in the vicinity of the power stations. Salt-laden prevailing winds often restrict the height and distort the shape of trees.

The active industrial sites are chiefly located around the harbour and nuclear power stations. There is still some activity at Middleton, including a new sewage treatment plant, but much of the area is derelict, planned to be part of a newly designated community woodland. A start has been made on this but its further establishment is very much dependent on suitable funding being found.

The river estuary and sea coast contain substantial areas of saltmarsh, both along the River Lune, between Overton and Sunderland Point, and at Middleton. Being subject to tidal encroachment these areas are largely as they always have been but old maps show that the salt marshes were much more extensive up to the early part of the twentieth century, before additional land was reclaimed by the building of further sea walls. In some places both the old and new sea defences can be identified.

Natural Heritage

Principles

Man and nature have always interacted. History shows how our actions have changed the environment and consequently the wildlife populations. Other forces not under our control also affect the balance of nature, and sometimes we do not understand why. The approach to our natural heritage supported here is succinctly and admirably enshrined in a Quaker booklet[1].

> We do not own the world and its riches are not ours to dispose of at will. Show a loving consideration for all creatures, and seek to maintain the beauty and variety of the world. Work to ensure that our increasing power over nature is used responsibly, with reverence for life.

An apparently opposite view is illustrated by a recent letter to a Devon newspaper by a farmer[2].

> I can proudly say that on my farm, that employs not only my family, but also four outside workers, there are no badgers, no rabbits, no mice, no snakes, no lizards, no rodents, and if I could stop the birds flying over I would. My farm produces food, not fluffy little animals. I am a farmer, not a zoo keeper!

Although this farmer (he may just have his tongue in his cheek) dislikes wildlife at least on his farm there are other farmers who are in principle sympathetic to wildlife; but the ways in which agricultural policies and practices have developed over the second half of the twentieth century have resulted in the environment in which they work being almost completely hostile to wildlife.

'Save Our Countryside' is a frequently seen slogan but an empty sentiment; many of the features of the countryside we used to enjoy have been destroyed by the combined forces of herbicides, pesticides and powerful machinery. Gone are the flower-rich hay meadows; herbicides drastically reduce the flora, leaving it largely confined to roadside verges. Pesticides destroy the insect and invertebrate populations which in turn has a knock on effect higher up the food chain. Powerful machinery enables greater domination of the land, hedges are either uprooted or reduced to minuscule versions of their former state, hardly flowering or regenerating, wet areas are drained and ponds polluted or filled in, and crops are grown winter and summer leaving no land fallow for wildlife to exploit. What is it that we are being asked to save? A green and pleasant land? Green certainly, but not very pleasant in terms of biodiversity. Edith Holden writing her diary[3] in 1906 would not recognise the countryside we have today. The defence that modern agricultural practices are an essential component of efficient production of food is now seriously questioned, for example in a brilliant analysis by Graham Harvey[4], an agricultural journalist and scriptwriter for The Archers. This is an extremely well documented account with many historical references; he likens the countryside to an industrial site, a bland, featureless and empty landscape.

However not all is necessarily lost; bodies such as the Farming and Wildlife Advisory Group encourage practices which allow for modern agricultural methods and wildlife to coexist. One example of coexistence is the Allerton Project[5], started in 1992 with an aim :

> ... to develop a system of profitable farming and land use which is compatible with the conservation of wild game and other wildlife.

Conservation organizations such as English Nature, the National Trust (creator of the first nature reserve at Wicken Fen, Cambridge in 1899), the Wildlife Trusts, Woodland Trust, and RSPB have for many years endeavoured to protect wildlife oases in the form of nature reserves, to preserve rare habitats and their associated species from extinction. They are now paying much greater attention to the wider countryside; it is now doubted whether a 'tidy' and sanitized countryside is either a sustainable or desirable policy for the future; it is further argued on good evidence that an environment lacking in biodiversity is not a healthy one. The Government is now on the way to subscribing to this view as this comment by the Director of the Royal Society for the Protection of Birds shows[7]:

> RSPB members have always known that birds in our gardens, countryside and wild places contribute enormously to the quality of life - now it is official. 'Number of birds' has been selected (by the Government) as the indicator of the state of UK wildlife. ... Birds are excellent indicators of the health of the environment. They occupy all habitats and are near the top of the food chain so that birds' well-being reflects what is happening to many other animals and plants right across the country. If bird numbers fall then the rest of biodiversity is probably suffering too. ... What does it mean for the health of the countryside when such common birds as the skylark, blackbird, house sparrow, starling, hedge sparrow and swallow have all declined? We fear that the bird index will decline in future unless the Government acts decisively. Our government must work to change the Common Agricultural Policy. At a time when farmers and farmland birds are both threatened we need a better system of support which rewards farmers for farming in a truly sustainable way; wheat and wildlife, beef and biodiversity should be what we are all trying to achieve from the countryside. ... Our message is that birds are an important indicator of the quality of life and that government can ensure that this indicator will rise.

People appear more conscious of birds than almost any other form of wildlife; many now comment on the absence of birds from their gardens and local fields, for example the disappearance of skylarks from much if not all of the peninsula, except for some small wintering flocks on the coast and a few nesting pairs on the currently

Natural Heritage

undisturbed grassland parts of Middleton Industrial Site. Birds are near the top of the food chain and their absence indicates what is happening down the chain. The RSPB is the second most well supported charity in the countryside; its conservation mission is based on the belief that birds and nature enrich people's lives, and that nature conservation is fundamental to a healthy environment on which the survival of the human race depends.

Wildlife sites

Heysham Harbour and Nature Reserve

The harbour was built at the beginning of the twentieth century over and south of the promontories Near Naze and Far Naze on the shore of Half Moon Bay. The tip of Near Naze and the remains of its lighthouse can still be seen off the north harbour wall by the helicopter pad. The walls of the harbour were built further out than the original land in order to access the deep water channel, labelled Heysham Lake on current Ordnance Survey maps.

Both before and after the building of the harbour this area was an important wildlife site; the building of the power stations from the late 1960s at first reduced the value of the site but, conscious of the traditions of the area, Nuclear Electric (now British Energy) designated part of their non-operational land as a nature reserve; this is now managed by Lancashire Wildlife Trust.

Full details about the area and the Reserve can be found in a reserve leaflet[6].

Heysham Nature Reserve now occupies the land in the bottom third of this map.
(Reproduced from the Ordnance Survey 25" to 1 mile map: First Edition 1891: Lancashire Sheet XXIX 16.)

Natural Heritage

The area is underlaid by St Bees sandstone which may be seen outcropping at Red Nab rocks to the south of the power stations; these rocks are the southern tip of a ridge from the Nazes along Heysham Banks (see map), which can still be seen to the east of the power stations; the Banks is a natural feature accentuated by man to protect the farm fields which used to be along Moneyclose Lane from incursion by high tides. Another lane, Banks Lane, of which little or no trace can be found now on the ground (though still shown in part on the OS 1:10,000 Town Map of Lancaster and Morecambe, 1990), used to run under the eastern side of the Banks to Banks House; along this lane older residents can recall seeing bee orchids flowering in June. Fortunately they have survived and, liking disturbed ground, have reappeared in good numbers on the plateau (a dump of excavated rock/clay) on the Reserve.

The construction of the harbour, involving a sea-defence wall from the west quay to Red Nab rocks, created a large stretch of brackish water and marsh to the west of the Banks. Because of its coastal location on a natural promontory in the relative shelter of Morecambe Bay this area attracted large numbers of sea-birds, waders and freshwater birds and it became a sanctuary for wintering sea ducks and swans. In addition Red Nab was a useful stopping off point for birds on one of the major migration routes in Western Europe. The lake was gradually reduced in size by developments linked to the harbour at Heysham, and when the construction of the Heysham Power stations began in the 1960s and the remainder was filled in to allow the construction of car parks and storage areas.

The present Nature Reserve is at the northern marshy end of the land to the east of the Banks. The scrub habitat that has developed provides valuable cover and food for insects and song birds. In 1985 in an attempt to arrest the natural succession from marsh to dry land, a small pond was excavated beneath the pylons.

Recording of wildlife around the harbour area has been done for many years by local enthusiasts; in recent years this has been done very thoroughly and systematically by the nature reserve warden and a group of volunteer helpers. Some unusual species of birds are ringed on migration; unusual species of butterfly, moth and dragonfly have also been noted in recent years.

There is still a wader roost at Red Nab on medium high tides; from there it is possible to walk along the sea wall to the lighthouse at the tip of the south harbour wall; the warm effluent water which is discharged from the power stations through outfall channels along this wall attracts fish and consequently gulls and terns (in season). Another more recent high tide roost has developed on the grass and sea-wall adjacent to the helicopter pad on the north harbour-wall; the waders seem to have realised that they are safe although lorries park nearby; dog walkers do not encroach on the pad, for obvious safety reasons.

Natural Heritage

Morecambe Bay

This is a site of international importance at times holding the largest concentration of wading birds anywhere in Britain. Heysham Harbour is one of the best vantage points around the bay from which to appreciate its vastness and observe the birds which live in and migrate through the bay. At times of strong onshore winds species normally seen only out in the Irish Sea are blown towards the coast.

The shore of the bay at Heysham has skears (remnants of glacial drumlins) which are exposed at low tide. In and around these are pools containing a wide variety of marine life.

The Bay is a vulnerable and disturbed habitat; waste and sewage which used to be pumped neat into the bay both diminished and attracted wildlife; records show that the cleaning up of the waste treatment in recent years is lowering the populations of some winter wildfowl. There has always been a variety of fishing activity around the harbour and skears; the beaches in the Village and Half Moon bays used to be busy in holiday periods during the first half of the century and are now regularly disturbed by residents and visitors walking their dogs.

Heysham Head and St Peter's Church

The Barrows field is now heavily used as amenity land with unrestricted public access; it was previously used as horse pasture for the Rectory and others and comparatively undisturbed. In spring it used to be carpeted with bluebells but these are now largely confined to the edges of the few remaining patches of coastal scrub. The cliffs and the wild area to the south (used as a go-kart track in the middle of the century as part of the Heysham Head pleasure park) have much more botanical and ornithological interest. In summer the gorse holds a good population of linnets and a few whitethroat; the cliffs, the only substantial ones in Lancashire, are largely inaccessible and have two unusual ferns, Royal Fern and Sea Spleenwort. The former used to be collected by Victorians for their gardens, thus denuding many wild populations; the latter only grows in shady rocky sites subject to sea spray.

The churchyard in spring is host to an uncommon plant, Meadow Saxifrage, and also the non-native Pink Purslane; churchyards generally are areas of unimproved grassland and when not over-manicured can be host to a good variety of plants.

Heysham Moss

Marsh Cinquefoil

This last remnant of the previously large area of mossland is very special and it is crucial for the rare plant species which it contains that its water content is not further reduced by continuing attempts at drainage of surrounding areas. It is also possibly under threat from more human disturbance from the new housing development on the other side of the railway. Currently Lancashire Wildlife Trust is negotiating to purchase much of the moss and its associated woodland. Plants include Bog Rosemary and Marsh Cinquefoil; the Grasshopper Warbler has occasionally bred.

Lune Estuary and Coastal saltmarsh

From Lancaster Tip to Sunderland Point the river is largely undisturbed except on occasions by jet-skis. In winter the mudflats and saltmarsh hold substantial numbers of waders and swans, sometimes including the wild Whooper and Bewick's Swans, joined occasionally by groups of Grey Lag and Pink Footed Geese. Up to the latter part of the twentieth century, before increasing high spring tide levels, there was a regular colony of breeding Common Terns near Bazil Point, Overton. In season the Overton and Middleton saltmarsh are in turn awash with Common Scurvy Grass, then Thrift and later Sea Aster; both have good breeding populations of Shelduck and Redshank. The inner shore-line along the Middleton saltmarsh holds some unusual species, flora and invertebrates.

Until the tree was severely damaged in a violent storm in 1998 Sunderland Point was home to a rare (female) Black Poplar, locally known as a cotton-tree because of the fleecy nature of its seeds. There is some regrowth from the relict stump. This tree is mentioned in Richard Mabey's *Flora Britannica*[8]. It is said to have come from America on a ship and to have been planted by the skipper but botanists are certain that this is a native tree *Populus nigra ssp. betulifolia*. Another Black Poplar can be found in Freeman's Wood across the Lune from Snatchems. The species is rare because it has difficulty in regenerating naturally now that so much of the wetland of Britain has been drained. It is amongst our oldest native species spanning some 10,000 years. An estimate of their current population is about 2000 and a scheme to regenerate them from cuttings taken from

Natural Heritage

existing trees began in 1994. Black Poplars appear in famous paintings such as Constable's *The Haywain*.

Middleton Industrial Site

There is a substantial pond and adjacent wet area on the northern side of the road to the new sewage treatment plant. This has recently created a lot of interest. The large Emperor dragonfly was first recorded there in the 1990s and is now also found on Heysham Nature Reserve. Other species new to the area have been Black and Ruddy Darter. The pond is the only breeding site of Little Grebe in the peninsula. Here we have a typical example of how wildlife moves in again when sites are disused and left undisturbed. The site will form part of the planned Middleton Wood.

General

Besides the specific sites already listed above there are many small unsanitized pockets in the peninsula where wildlife still thrives. There are reedy dikes around Middleton and Overton, a small number of field ponds, old quarries and marl-pits once used for the extraction of marl to fertilize the land.

Some wildlife pockets are gardens where the gardener is wildlife conscious and does not readily resort to the use of chemicals and machinery in the interests of 'tidiness'. There is one site in Heysham, and probably more, where cowslips and the rare Adder's Tongue Fern are thriving in a lawn, presumably surviving from the pasture that preceded the garden.

A full flora survey of the whole of Lancaster District was published in the 1980s and this is a very useful checklist[9]. Annual bird reports and ten year check-lists published by the Lancaster and District Birdwatching Society contain full details of records in the area from the 1950s onwards.

References

1. *Advices and Queries*: issued by the Society of Friends. Quoted in The Guardian, 24 April 1999, by Alison Leonard.
2. Letter to the North Devon Journal from C Roberts, Black Torrington, Devon: April 1999. Quoted in Private Eye, no. 974, April 1999
3. Edith Holden : *The Country Diary of an Edwardian Lady* : Michael Joseph 1977
4. Graham Harvey : *The Killing of the Countryside* : Jonathan Cape 1997
5. N Boatman & C Stoate : *Arable farming and wildlife - Can they coexist?* : British Wildlife Vol 10, no. 4, April 1999
6. *Guide to Heysham Nature Reserve* : Lancashire Wildlife Trust/British Energy
7. Extracts from *Comment* by Graham Wynne, RSPB Chief Executive : *Birds* : Spring 1999
8. Richard Mabey : *Flora Britannica* (p. 135) : Sinclair-Stevenson 1996
9. L A & P D Livermore : *The Flowering Plants and Ferns of North Lancashire* : 1987

Heysham Peninsula
3. St Patrick *(c.386 - c.461)* and St Patrick's Chapel

There are several Myths about St Patrick, of which this is a compilation[1]:

Once upon a time, Patrick was an Irishman who converted the people of Ireland, and founded churches and monasteries. For this he was canonised St Patrick, and the Irish adopted him as their patron Saint.

St Patrick then set out to convert North West England. His boat landed on a sandbank at Heysham (St Patrick's Skear). He came ashore and built a church, the present St Patrick's Chapel. He then moved through North Lancashire and Cumbria converting the people and founding churches. He also performed miracles, such as striking springs of water.

On his death St Patrick was buried in the first of the rock-hewn graves, followed by his principal successors. Later generations built the church, with graveyard; and gradually the chapel fell into disuse.

The main problem with the myths is that Patrick died about 461, and the chapel appears to date later. Nevertheless, myths are often a clue to some underlying events.

Once Patrick had arrived in Ireland, appointed missionary bishop about 432 he did not return to Britain. He had such trouble with his bishops there that he was not able to return, and this is described in his *Confessions*. If he was ever in Heysham it would be before his return to Ireland, and it has been suggested that he may have come with a few followers from York.

St Patrick's Chapel

St Patrick's Chapel

Monsignor Gradwell, an historian of the last century, and much quoted by Whewell Hogarth, insists that St Patrick came to Heysham. He offers no real evidence, and modern historians doubt that this could be so:

> Strange as it may appear it is certain that he landed on our shores, and traversed our hills and dales; that he left on the very soil indelible marks of his presence, and that a pilgrimage was established in his honour by the devout Irish people, which endured for a 1000 years and of which we can find traces to this day.
>
> Morecambe Bay and its winding coast are studded with sites consecrated by his presence and wondrous deeds. Even before the sailor touches the land, St Patrick's Skear is pointed out to him. When he reaches the rocky shore and lands at Heysham, St Patrick's Chapel attracts his attention, and as he journeys northwards he finds himself passing St Patrick's Well, Slyne ...
>
> ... The first is a view of the ruined chapel at Heysham, known as St Patrick's Chapel ... The architecture is extremely rude, and the masonry is equally so, for the building is of great antiquity. It has been exposed to all the inclemencies of the weather for about 1300 years, and so exhibits a time-worn and storm tossed appearance. At the close of the fourth century, in the year 394, a fugitive slave from Ireland had been driven by the wind and waves into Morecambe Bay. He landed near Heysham; and such was the veneration which, as time went on, grew up in the minds of the inhabitants of the coast for this apparently forlorn stranger that they built a chapel in his honour, and styled it by his name, the Chapel of St Patrick ...

Archaeological Investigation.

In 1977-78 there was a thorough investigation by Potter and Andrews from Lancaster University. Their findings were published in the Antiquaries Journal[2]. They found among other things that the chapel and the surrounding area had been used as a burial ground. About 85 sets of bones were found, of both sexes and all ages. Most had died by the age of 45, normal for the period. The bones (carbon-dated) were from about 1000 - 1200 AD.

The rock-cut graves are more difficult to date. Whilst man has grown in stature over the centuries, these rock-cut graves are still not big enough to contain bodies. It is more likely that they were ossuaries, receptacles for placing bones only. There are seven in the western group and some have a socket for a cross and are rebated to take a grave cover. The crosses and grave slabs were removed long ago.

The dig was not popular with the villagers. They had always known that the area was a burial ground, but as the land belonged to the rectory, people were normally not allowed to wander in the area, except at holiday times and therefore under supervision. It was only with greater public

St Patrick's Chapel

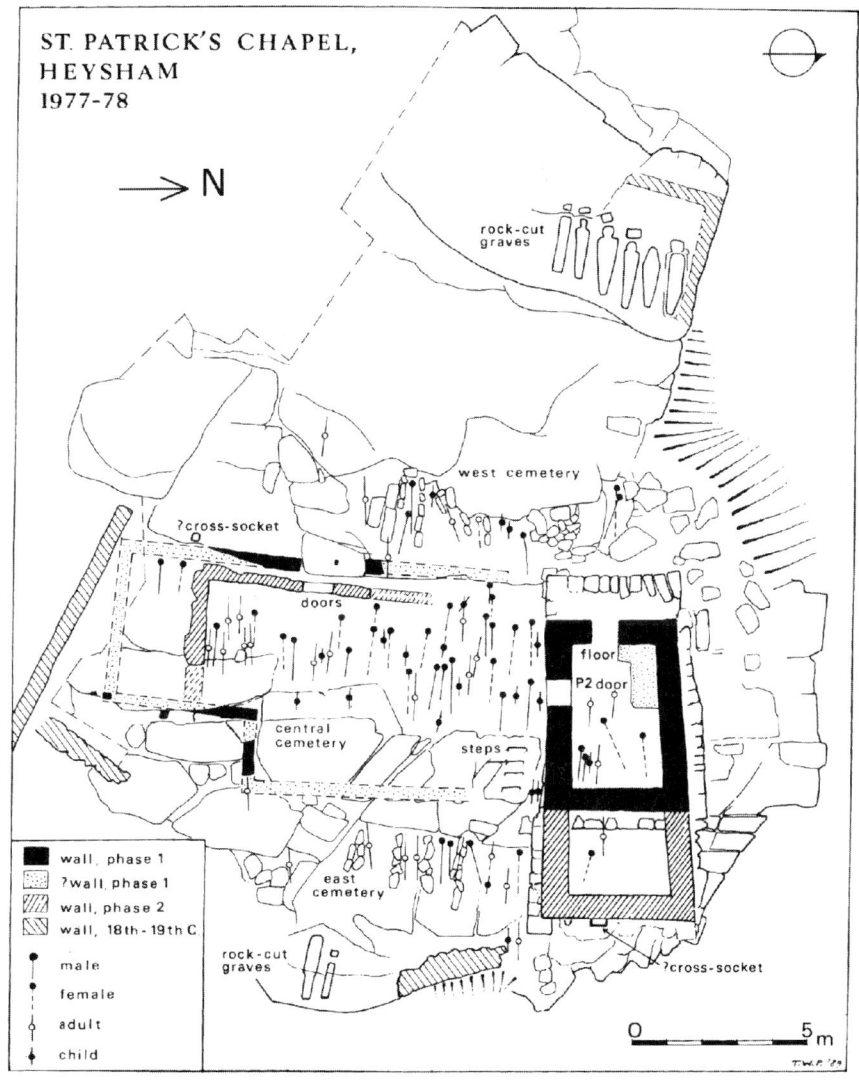

St Patrick's Chapel and cemetery
General plan of the excavations

access that erosion uncovered the bones and led to the 'dig'. The bones, after examination, were left in a workman's hut in plastic bin bags, but after a local outcry were re-buried in St Peter's churchyard. A memorial cross covers their final resting place.

References
1. J C Procter : *St Patrick's Chapel* : Heysham Heritage Association 1997
2. T W Potter and R D Andrews : *Excavation and Survey at St Patrick's Chapel and St Peter's Church, Heysham, 1977-78* : Antiquaries Journal Vol LXXIV 1994

Heysham Peninsula
4. St Peter's Church

A postcard from the early 20th century

If St Peter's is the oldest Celtic Church in Lancashire, then it must have been in existence long before the estimated date of its millennium, held in 1967. The Celtic and Roman churches combined at the Synod of Whitby, AD664, and from that time Roman practices ruled. Is it possible therefore that there was a church on the site before that date?

It has been thought that St Patrick's Chapel and the original St Peter's Church, which may have been wooden and barn-like, are of similar date. If we take St Patrick's as about 5th century (*the century varies according to the historian*) then the original foundations of St Peter's would be of about the same period.

In 1977/8 at the time of the first archaeological dig at St Patrick's Chapel, the archaeologists wished to dig under the foundations of St Peter's. The Bishop came along to a Parochial Church Council (PCC) meeting in an effort to support the wishes of the experts, but the PCC decided that they would not allow disturbance to the foundations of the church. There was also a certain amount of anger in the village as the bones from the dig had not been dealt with sensitively. (*They had reportedly been left in a bin-liner in a derelict building.*) There is a small cross at the west side of the churchyard where the final interment took place.

St Peter's Church

West door

The west doorway, which is blocked up, is Anglo-Saxon in origin. The floor of the church is much higher inside than outside, and is flagged. Originally the floor inside the church would have been compacted earth. Was there once a rush-bearing ceremony to cover the floor with clean rushes once a year? The chancel archway is perhaps the oldest part of the church. The rope moulding decoration tells us this. The apse would be behind the arch. The aisles, the chancel and the side extensions are all of later dates, 13th to 16th century.

The small west window just inside the main door is the oldest, but it is not in situ. The internal unglazed window overlooking the chancel would originally be glazed and on an outside wall. One can still see the rebates for the frame. Most of the other windows are from the Victorian period, and some are dated.

During the last century, in 1864, the north aisle was built and two galleries removed from the north wall. The outline of one of the gallery doors can be seen on the west wall. The whitewash was removed from the outer walls at the same time. During renovations an Anglo-Saxon archway was discovered in the north wall. The Rector of the time, Rev John Royds, had the archway rebuilt, stone for stone, in the churchyard. At the same time human remains, he presumed of a previous Rector, were found under the chancel. In the coffin there had been a chalice of lead or lateen. This chalice, which is rather crumbly, is set into the wall on the south aisle. The bones were kept in a box in Mr Royds' study, and after his death interred inside the church under the chalice.

Rebuilt Anglo-Saxon Arch

St Peter's Church

The pews in the chancel, now occupied by the choir, were previously occupied by, on the left facing the altar, the rector's family and servants. Opposite sat two of the most prominent families in the area. These pews were the most expensive, in days when pews had to be paid for. The occupiers of the gallery pews were also among the few wealthier families.

The Royds family were rectors in Heysham for more than a hundred years, and even when there was no suitable successor they continued as patrons of the advowson (*right of patronage, to appoint a suitable incumbent*).

Because the parishioners have memories of the Royds family it has probably been forgotten that the Clarkson family reigned as rectors for nearly the same length of time. On the death of one rector the next Thomas Clarkson would be trained in another parish ready to take over in Heysham a few years later. It was during one of these breaks, whilst Reverend Thomas Clarkson was curate at Hornby, that Reverend Thomas Dunham Whitaker became rector at Heysham for about five years. He already held the vicarage at Whalley and he was later to become Vicar of Blackburn, of the church which is now the cathedral. He was an absentee vicar most of the time, and especially here at Heysham (*See Chapter 5*).

Inside the church can be found evidence of the long past. The 'crusader's tomb' on the west wall, is a lovely carved foliated cross.

The small south door inside the chancel has a lintel re-cycled from a gravestone. There are some old gravestones on the internal south wall, which were probably once outside. William Ward's memorial near the east windows is curious. (*Did he really make a tunnel from the Old Rectory under the chancel, as reported?*) The wooden screen dividing the chancel from the nave may once have been in Cockersand Abbey.

The hogback stone in the south aisle is a real treasure. This stone is not unique - there are others in Penrith churchyard and other towns towards the Scottish border - but it is probably the best. It had been outside, and the story is that it was buried, but no one remembers. What they do remember is that it was near to the sundial and it was decided to bring it indoors. The archaeologists again wished to examine it more closely at the university laboratory and two of the villagers decided this would not do and brought it inside the church. They could not tolerate anyone 'experts or not' getting to work on it with a chisel!

The Churchyard

There is the base of an Anglo-Saxon cross at the entrance to the churchyard. The top of the cross was probably used to support the porch. Carvings can be seen on the stones of the porch which match the cross. The main carving on the base is probably of Lazarus in his grave-clothes,

St Peter's Church

Cross base

and on another side is a haloed figure, which in certain lights looks like mother and child. This cross has given rise to a lot of speculation.

Also in the graveyard are some eleventh to thirteenth century grave covers, mostly covered in moss and level with the grass. These are to the south west of the church building and are not immediately seen, but are fairly close to the main path.

In the further south west corner is the Anglo-Saxon archway mentioned before.

The earliest grave with a memorial stone is of the early 1700s on the east side of the church, and other graves of the period are close to the church. The flat topped graves are earlier than those with an upright stone. The lower graveyard nearest the sea was opened in 1903 and was quickly filled. The sea wall has been washed away in the past. Graves on the west side with railing surrounds are mainly 19th century.

On the whole the memorial stones remain simple, without angels or urns, and the atmosphere is one of timelessness and tranquility. The modern part of the churchyard is on the east side, and there is a memorial garden - now closed, but bearing some interesting inscriptions - for the burial of ashes.

The Glebe Garden, to the south east, has been recovered from dereliction in the past few years, and is a quiet tribute to those who created it.

Heysham Peninsula
5. *They came to Heysham*

J M W Turner RA 1775 - 1851
Rev Dr T D Whitaker Ll D 1759 - 1821

J M W Turner visited Heysham during August 1816. We know he came because he made sketches possibly from the spot we now call 'Turner's View', close to the end of Knowlys Road, now somewhat obscured by brambles, from which in 1818 in his London studios he painted a picture of Heysham with the Cumbrian Hills in the background, *Heysham and Cumberland Mountains*.

It has been suggested that Turner stayed a night or so at the house called variously the Old Rectory, the Rectory, or Greese Cottage, which is at the bottom of Main Street and to the east of the church. This could not possibly have been so.

The historian Rev Dr Thomas Dunham Whitaker and Rector of Heysham at this time, friend of Turner, writes in *A History of Richmondshire*:

> Opposite to the church on the south side is the rectory, an irregular building, of which the oldest and meanest part was built by Mr Bushell, rector in the latter end of the seventeenth century ...
>
> Above the rectory begins a line of perpendicular rock, which shelters both that and the village at once from the sun and the storms ...

Is it likely that Turner would have been invited to spend even a night in a 'mean' house when there was a suitable inn, the Royal, to accommodate him?

The fine building of Greese Cottage is well documented. It was built by the Rector of the time, said to be William Ward MA, who was Rector from 1636, with a break, until at least 1650, and probably until his death in 1670. This Rectory house was taken over by the Clarkson family who had a long reign as rectors of the parish; in this case the date over the lintel (1688) would be inaccurate, and quite a few years too late. There is a carved beam inside the house giving an earlier date.

A BIT OF LOWER HEYSHAM.

Greese Cottage in 1898

The Rectory that T D Whitaker encountered was 'south' of the church, that is, in the same position, or parallel to, the present Rectory. That could make it the original part of the Bushell's rectory building demolished in the 1960s. That particular building had many additions and extensions and there are drawings and photographs in existence. The first structure could very well have been 'mean'. As Dr Whitaker was an absentee Rector it is not very likely he took frequent advantage of its shelter.

During the year of Turner's visit, 1816, there was a total of about a hundred christenings, marriages and burials of which Whitaker conducted about ten per cent, and none of those during August at the time of Turner's visit.

What is likely is that Turner came down to Lancaster via Crook o'Lune where he also made sketches for a later picture, spent the night at Lancaster, probably at the King's Arms, then made his way to Heysham, where he spent the morning sketching, returning to the King's Arms in the evening for his supper. He may indeed have had time for a foaming tankard and a pie at the Royal, but he sketched so rapidly that he did not need much time in Heysham.

Whitaker was by way of being Turner's sponsor during his early struggling years. Turner had contracted to provide the etchings which illustrate *A History of Richmondshire*. There should have been about a hundred and twenty five altogether, but Turner had an increasing work load, or got bored with the project when he could not find suitable engravers, and did only twenty drawings from which engravings were made.

Also, as said before, Whitaker was an absentee Rector. He much preferred to spend time in his own village Holme-in-Cliviger where he was perpetual curate, or in Whalley where he was also Vicar - again an absentee - leaving his son in place as curate until his son's death at the age of 23.

He was offered the Vicarage of Blackburn - later to become the Bishopric - towards the end of his term of office in Heysham, and he died only a short time later.

Absentee Rectors

It is not suggested that Dr Whitaker was doing anything he should not in being an absentee rector. It was customary for men of wealth who were in Holy Orders to employ curates to minister on their behalf. The Rector received the income from the parish, from the tenants and farmers, and paid the stipend of the curate. It is unlikely that the poor people of the parish contributed money to the church. Tithing was still the norm. If they were able to pay in money they did so, but it was more likely to be in 'kind' or in the form of manual labour.

They came to Heysham

Whitaker as Rector and Historian

One wonders whether Whitaker was really aware of the village and the villagers. He writes :

> Of this parish it is remarkable, that there is no market, no shop, and, till the last year, no butcher; no medical practitioner, no attorney, no endowed school, no sea-boat, and, thanks to the want of water, no manufactory ... in the whole parish there is not a spring of clear and tasteless water, the wells being mere puddles, and those too rendered brackish, by some secret communication with the sea through crevices in the rocks.

The parish records show that a school had been mooted as early as 1769 and in 1812 there was a deed endowing the school. Had the school gone out of existence in the meantime or had Whitaker not been aware of it? Was a sea-boat needed where a horse and cart could do the work of shell-fish catching? And walking out at low tide to remove fish from the baulks made a boat unnecessary.

His contribution to history, *A History of Whalley* and *A History of Richmondshire* are well known, but he also had a contribution to the environment. He planted thousands of trees near his mansion at Holme; it was said that many of them were to hide the railway! On his death his coffin was made from a mature larch which he had planted himself.

He was a critic of the social and environmental effects of the Industrial Revolution.

Ruskin and Turner

Ruskin was a great admirer of Turner and came to Heysham following in Turner's footsteps. As with Whitaker he had ideas concerning the effects of the Industrial Revolution and deplored the destruction of the environment for profit.

When he came to Heysham he stayed at Salem Farm, just below Turner's View in a room overlooking the sea. He writes of Turner's painting *Heysham and Cumberland Mountains* with reference to Heysham, and gives a description of the village at that time, through Turner's eyes.

Ruskin's visit would be after the death of J M W Turner in 1851 and before his own lapse into mental illness in 1870. 1865 is the most probably date of his sojourn in Heysham, and in August of that year.

> Perhaps Heysham ... which as to its locality may be considered a companion to ... Lancaster Sands, presents as interesting an example as we could find of Turner's feelings ...
> The subject is a simple north-country village, on the shore of Morecambe Bay; not in the common sense a picturesque village; there are no pretty bow-windows, or red roofs, or rocky steps of entrance to the rustic doors, or quaint gables; nothing but a single street of thatched and chiefly

clay-built cottages, ranged in a somewhat monotonous line, the roofs so green with moss that at first we hardly discern the houses from the fields and trees.

The village street is closed at one end by a wooden gate, indicating the little traffic there is on the road through it, and giving it something the look of a large farmstead, in which a right of way lies through the yard. The road which leads to this gate is full of ruts, and winds down a bad bit of hill between two broken banks of moor ground, succeeding immediately to the few enclosures which surround the village; they can hardly be called gardens, but a decayed fragment of fencing fills the gaps in the bank ... At the end of the village is a better house, with three chimneys and a dormer window in its roof, and the roof is of shingle instead of thatch, very rough. This house is no doubt the clergyman's; there is some smoke from one of its chimneys, none from any other in the village ...
All noble composition of this kind can be reached only by instinct ...

Whilst one must agree with all Ruskin writes, one wonders whether the Heyshamers of this time would recognise themselves. They would be likely to recognise Turner's portrait, but perhaps not Ruskin's description of the picture. Ruskin has allowed his emotions to take over so that he fails to be objective.

Ruskin was something of a prude, even for the times he lived in. In trying to protect Turner from criticism he was instrumental in having some of Turner's paintings destroyed, this particularly applied to Turner's nudes. For that Ruskin has a lot to answer for.

William Woodhouse 1857 - 1939.

William Woodhouse, the well-known local artist, was born at a house in Morecambe Street, Poulton-le-Sands in October 1857.

He first showed his talents as an artist at the age of five, for during prayers at Sunday School he would scratch out pictures of animals and birds with a pin on his desk.

He attended the National School, Morecambe, where he amazed his teachers by his exquisite drawing. Later, he attended art classes at the Mechanics' Institute in Lancaster to which he used to walk. Although he had some art training his art work was practically wholly self taught.

While still a young lad his drawing and paintings of animals, birds, and local country scenes were soon in demand by local people. Eventually, animal lovers from all over the country were commissioning him to paint pictures of their favourite dog or horse. Now recognised, his works in oils, water-colour and drawing became more and more collectable and still are today.

They came to Heysham

Heysham in Winter
William Woodhouse : Haworth Art Gallery, Accrington

He exhibited his work all over the country: London, Edinburgh, Liverpool, Preston, and Lancaster. His work was accepted by the Royal Academy, the Royal Scottish Academy, and the Royal Institute of Painters in Water Colours. In 1931, from 9 June to 22 July at the Storey Institute, an exhibition was held of

> Oils, Water Colours, Etchings and Dry Paints by William Woodhouse and his son Ronald Basil Emsley Woodhouse.

There were 256 exhibits, of which 191 were by William.

William and his wife, Maria Elizabeth, née Emsley, had two children, Ronald (Roy) who was also making his name as an artist, and Winifred (Winnie).

William Woodhouse moved his studio to various locations in Morecambe, but in 1902 he moved to 8 Furness Road, Cross Cop, Heysham, the district he knew and loved best. It was in his studio at this house that he produced some of his best work.

In early January 1939 at the age of 81, William Woodhouse passed away. His interment was at Heysham Parish churchyard and the Rector, Canon C C T Royds, officiated.

We must be thankful for the legacy of wonderful paintings which he has left for us. Some of these are in the Lancaster Museum's Art Collection.

Heysham Peninsula

6. *Heysham Harbour* (Some cuttings from the newspapers)

2nd February 1898, Morecambe Visitor

Progress of the Work
A Visit to Klondyke & Dawson City[1]

'Hotel' with Stores and Police Station behind

'Klondyke Clothing Stores', 'Klondyke Butchery', the barber's shop and the Klondyke Police Station, the two last being cheek by jowl. It is Klondyke, Klondyke everywhere, except just across the hill there, where another canteen opens its doors and which is built in the centre of Dawson City.

It is only a few months since Messrs Price and Wills commenced their gigantic undertaking, but what tremendous progress has been made. Plant has been rolling up on to the scene day by day until the place now resembles an engineering works and timber yard combined. Well-made huts for the housing of navvies have sprung up like mushrooms in the heart of the Klondyke, and further away there is quite a colony of married folks occupying comfortable

Whatever Heysham may be in the future and the probabilities are that it will become a shipping port of no unpretentious character, it is hardly likely that it will ever be able to shake off the pseudonym of Klondyke by which it is known far and near. 'Klondyke Hotel' proclaims itself to the resident navvy when he has finished his daily toil, and to the casual visitor intent on having a look round, in bold white letters shaded in blue, from the gable end of the canteen.

Close at hand 'Klondyke Bakery' holds up its head towering high above

Stores, Police Station and Bakery
(Heysham Banks is in the background)

- 25 -

Heysham Harbour

Construction of Heysham Harbour

looking houses erected apparently with a strict regard to the building line.

Engine sheds are being built in close proximity to the offices of the contractors, where the pay is doled out Saturday by Saturday and near which is the pay box occupied every Saturday by the postmaster of Heysham to oblige those thrifty navvies and other workmen who desire to place a part of their hard earned wages in Her Majesty's Savings Bank. Up to the present moment there has been

No Inordinate Rush

for the Savings Bank, the bulk of the men making for Klondyke Hotel as soon as their pockets have been lined, and only leaving behind here and there a depositor to interview Mr Clarke.

Mr Furness, the agent for Messrs Price & Wills, has now something like 200 men at work, and this number will gradually be increased until the figure reaches 2,000 or thereabouts. At the Near Naze promontory the work of forming the initial portion of the great breakwater is proceeding apace. Metals have been laid around the hill which has to be removed, engines are running backwards and forwards with full wagons to be emptied, and empty wagons to be filled. Here it is mostly spade work, though further on the presence of sandstone rock necessitates blasting operations. This great arm into the sea which has just been commenced will be one mile in length and right across the intended harbour stretching from Red Nab to meet the one from Near Naze, will be another breakwater one and a half miles in length. That too has already been commenced, and a couple of engines are engaged in drawing the wagons.

Whilst excavations were in progress at the seaward end of North wharf, a prehistoric relic was round. Beneath a bed of peat one foot thick, 30 feet below the Ordnance Datum Line, and 37 feet beneath the sand, part of the skull and horns of the European Bison was found. This relic was, in 1901, the only proof that this animal once existed in this country ... This relic was presented to Lancaster Museum in 1916 together with a detailed scale drawing by Frank Casson.

Heysham Harbour

The steam navvies are at work

Ripping and Tearing

at the hillside which by and by will have disappeared, two million cubic yards in all, and have been transferred to form the breakwater which will protect the harbour.

There is method and a system pervading the whole works which cannot fail to strike even the most unobservant onlooker, and a discipline, clear and defined, which must leave its mark behind.

Whilst the harbour works are proceeding so satisfactorily and so rapidly, Messrs Godfrey and Liddelow are pushing towards the completion of the line which branches off from the main line near Morecambe and will run right on to the pier to be constructed in the harbour, and which will extend to deep water.

--oOo--

Navvies earned about 5/- a day according to a schedule, and the rate was increased as more labourers were needed for the harbour or railway. These wages were fairly high at a time when £1 a week was considered a reasonable wage for a man. Skilled men, fitters, carpenters, blacksmiths, bricklayers, earned far more than this: 10/- or 8s 6d a day.

The Klondyke Bakery produced up to 600 loaves daily. Being able to eat and drink like a navvy was a pre-requisite. Two pounds of beef and a gallon of beer a day was accepted as the norm.

2nd February 1898
Extract from The Visitor

There were continuous reports of silting. Official denial came through the Yorkshire Post of difficulties due to the silting up of the sand to the harbour entrance - Baldwin Bent, resident engineer on the works reported that :

"There is no foundation whatever for the report that unexpected difficulty has arisen due to any sand silting up as stated. Some months ago the contractors purposely caused this sand to silt alongside their temporary jetty so that the vessels bringing sand and cement to the works might take the ground on a good bed at low water. Groynes have also been put out at right angles at the other embankments to prevent scour along the toe. These have caused sand to accumulate between them as was expected, and desired, and it is difficult to understand how the report arose."

14th September 1900,
Morecambe & District Gazette

SPORTS AT HEYSHAM
A regular Gala Day

A happy idea ... two or three residents of Heysham, was to organise village sports, and no sooner was the idea mooted than it was taken up with a great deal of enthusiasm ... as the outcome of the most successful athletic festival was held on Saturday in the field directly opposite the

Heysham Harbour

National School at Higher Heysham. Councillor James Harrison and Mr Roland Willacy may be described as the primary movers in the matter, and the first named acted as Chairman of Committee and Treasurer, and Mr Willacy as Secretary. The committee were councillors John Clark and R. Mashiter, Messrs John Mashiter, Robert Farr, Thomas Willacy, Thomas Wilson, Adam Parr, Fred Wade, James Clark, William Clark, Richard Sandham, James Parr, and Richard Stevenson.

Rev C T Royds, Mrs Grafton, Mr W E Tomlinson MP, Councillors F W Tattersall, John Clark, James Harrison and R Mashiter, Mr Fitzgibbon and Mr R B Lee were among the subscribers, and indeed - nearly every villager figured on the list, the Heysham Brass Band feeling the importance of the occasion ... gave their services, and soon after one o'clock met in the square where the inhabitants young and old gathered round them ... and afterwards marched in procession through Higher and Lower Heysham and then on to the field which had been admirably prepared for the occasion.

The programme consisted of no fewer than 25 events, and although a punctual start was made at two o'clock it was half past eight before the proceedings were concluded.

The youngsters were especially catered for, and the winners were ... proud of their brooches, Waterbury watches and other such articles.

Money prizes, ranging from ten shillings to fifteen shillings, were given to the seniors and the most successful competitor proved to be a digger from Klondyke whose name is still unknown to the promoters of the festival, but who in the days gone by has undoubtedly been a shining light on the track. He won the 200 yards readily enough, and secure in the running long jump, finishing second in the half mile race, in which he conceded the other competitors a big start, and wound up by winning the mile race with the greatest of ease. The old veterans turned out in full force over the 300 yards course; Councillor James Harrison showed a clean pair of heels.

The consequence of the success which attended the sports was that it is intended to make the affair an annual institution and to hold it earlier in the season.

The contractors and landlords of the canteens organised other sports days. Mr William Mitchell, the Lancaster Brewer subscribed a 'five pound note' and about £30 was offered in prizes at the Klondyke sports in which 600 navvies took part.

Flags and bannerettes were gaily floating in the breeze from the crown of the hill ... Those who had Sunday Best donned it ... In the forenoon the inhabitants turned to witness a cricket match, between the Klondyke Flutterers and the Red Nab Warriors.

As the end of match score was Flutterers 37, Warriors 22, the match could not have been memorable. It was followed by the sports which took place in a drizzle, but which were widely reported in the press.

--oOo--

With such a large number of men employed on building the harbour, it was inevitable that there was the occasional accident.

26th October

Terrible fatality at Klondyke

The inquest ... every precaution against accidents ... nobody to blame. The funeral of Thomas Barber, whose sad death occurred last Wednesday morning at Heysham Harbour Works ... was held in a little wooden mission room at Klondyke on Thursday afternoon before Mr R Holden. This was the first fatality that had happened at these works, which was a matter of wonder when there were five and sometimes seven hundred men employed there upon work of a complicated nature.

(*He was apparently killed by a large stone which rolled down a hill and fell on his neck.*)

25th September 1900

Terrible accident at Klondyke
One man killed and another injured.

Engaged in shunting operations. Terrible crush between buffers and wagons.

The other unfortunate man James O'Donnel was thought to be less severely injured and was removed to his lodgings in Dawson City. The poor fellow however must have been badly crushed because after lingering some time he expired in spite of all that Doctor Hogarth could do for him. (*His landlady gave evidence at the inquest.*)

(*Dr Hogarth was Dr Bertram Hogarth, uncle to the historian Dr Whewell Hogarth. They were said not to like each other much.*)

6th November 1900

Saturday's Police Court
A Klondyke incident

Prosecutor said that at 1.45 in the afternoon of 22nd ult. the defendant struck him in the face without any provocation, and having a ring on his finger, inflicted such injuries that he had to be attended by Dr Hogarth. The defendant called out that he was objecting to the ring. The case appears to be six of one ... and was dismissed.

You could guarantee every Sunday there would be a bare fisted fight at Klondyke - because it was all sand. They would get drunk on a Saturday night and fall out. There was a gang of them. They would go to Sunday School, (the local children) then when they were let out they used to run along Barrows Lane to see the fight. Village bobby used to ride his bicycle and referee. Monday morning they were the best of pals.

Heysham Harbour

Midland Railway Dock at the completed Harbour

14th August 1901

Reported by the **Midland Railway Company**, according to the daily paper, are spending a heap of money at Heysham on constructing the Harbour works. By this time one has become accustomed both to the harbour works and to the report in the daily papers, but it isn't every day that we hear such a statement as that made by the Midland Railway Company at the half yearly meeting held the other day. He told the higher shareholders that the harbour works were going on well and would be completed by the end of next year. Already **£270,000** has been spent on the works and there still remains a trifling sum of **£228,000** yet to be paid to the navvies etc. before the contractors Messrs Price and Wills are finished.

It was no use going on the site unless you had a navvy shovel, and he (Joe Steel, Blacksmith) always kept about 250 shovels in the building. A shovel was 1s. 6d. Well, at that time there was Heysham Harbour being built, Immingham Docks, and Barry Docks in Wales, all at the same time. They'd buy these shovels, and if they got sacked on one gang they'd join another gang. Some of 'em used to get fed up after they'd been working a good while, and bring the shovel back, and he used to given 'em 9d. and he used to refurbish 'em, you know, put another steel plate in ...

--oOo--

Even the wives could be quarrelsome!

28th August 1901

Mary Jane Teasdale lives at Dawson City. She is a lady built on very generous proportions and at the Castle on Saturday

- 30 -

she just about filled the witness box in order to prefer a charge of using threats against a diminutive young woman named Nelly Benson, also a resident of the famous City. She refused to say, but had it written down what had been said, but as she could neither read nor write we don't really know what she had said. Benson was bound over, in the sum of £5 to keep the peace for six months. She had apparently been in the habit of coming to listen at the window of their hut at night. The next morning when the defendant was along she came to abuse her about what she had said ... "I have not a soul on the field to defend me" pathetically added the defendant ...

16th October 1901 : 'Cuckoo' (Gazette Reporter)

Many of the employees of the Harbour works reside at Sandylands and for their convenience Mr Tomlinson the manager of the omnibus company has put on conveyances to take them backwards and forwards morning and evening at a weekly charge of 2/- for the double journey. Isn't that enough to make you wish you worked at Klondyke. Fancy going to your daily toil in a carriage and pair at two bob a week. Good old Klondyke.

---oOo---

Gas, Water and Electricity

All the buildings with the exception of the huts, were lighted by acetyline gas. When in full swing there were about 700 men living in this settlement.

Water Supply: Water is obtained by means of an artesian pump made by Messrs Timmins. The pump head well is 8 ft in internal diameter ... To prevent any surface pollution percolating into the borehole ... The pump is capable of delivering 28,000 gallons of water per day through a six inch main 1,550 yards in length into a reservoir of 92,850 gallons capacity, 38 feet above the rail level of the harbour ...

Electricity ... used for practically all the machinery ... is economical in working compared with hydraulic and steam power for the actuation of the cranes, capstans, lifts, pumps etc, ... imparts an elasticity to the power distribution scheme otherwise unobtainable. (*Harbour Engineer*)

---oOo---

Also with an increasing population there was the inevitable problem of **Sewerage**. Nothing changes!

7th December 1899

A letter from the Rev C T Royds reproof to the council for the insanitary conditions of Dawson City - the frightful and abominable stenches.

30th October 1900
to Dr Bertram Hogarth, Public Health

Sanitary Matters

"Many places which could be improved upon, certain old insanitary property, and to certain new property which have their cellars permanently flooded; both these conditions tend to the development of disease, and will not increase the district either residential or commercially. On these grounds I respectfully ask you to be strict in the way all building foundations, sites, etc, to be prepared and to insist on proper damp courses being made.

Scavenging

I have to thank you for the progress that has been made so far in this department. The purchase of a horse and covered cart and the engagement permanently of a man whose chief work will be the more frequent removal of refuse shows the interest you have taken in this department.

The middens, privies, ashpits especially in summer ought to be emptied and cleaned in the evenings, and no accumulation allowed to occur, and everything of a combustible nature ought to be burned.

I would again call your attention to the custom of throwing various kinds of rubbish, such as tinned meat or fruit tins, cabbage stalks etc. into the rear of buildings, especially at Dawson City and the back streets and ditches of the Battery estates.

Drains

All the new ones, when being laid ought to be tested and inspected. I would also recommend that the sewers be also periodically tested as to their efficiency, in keeping out the tidal water and sewage effluvia.

Disinfectation

... Committee being set up to select a site on which to build an isolation hospital, and ask them to consider at the same time a disinfecting station where bedding, clothing etc. could be disinfected."

19th October 1901

Heysham Sewerage Scheme

Over £1000 wanted, a big bill of extras.

18th November 1901

... Use of bottles to discover where the sewerage went. Hope for spirit of compromise.
Sewerage to be emptied into Heysham Lake and not near mussel beds.

26th November 1901

Morecambe Sewerage Scheme

Question seems to be whether Heysham mussel beds which are about a mile away from the outfall of the treated sewage at a place called Seldom Seen ... are affected.

> There was coal boats. I worked some one year. They run for 13 weeks. You started at one o'clock. There were two shifts. You never knew what time you were going to finish ... On a Saturday they had to do two trips to the Isle of Man.

Heysham Harbour

17 September 1902

Collision of two vessels in the early hours of Saturday morning. The Bell Rock and Blue Bell, the latter vessel laden with 600 tons of cement from Antwerp. The Bell Rock laden with ballast from Barrow cut the other boat amidships. The Blue Bell has been lifted, but the cement is of course useless.

17 September 1902, Gazette : 'Cuckoo'

Robert Shepherd the Klondyke navvy has been awarded a bronze medal by the Royal Humane Society for his courageous act of saving the life of a boy named Hanson during the recent gale at Heysham. Shepherd, it will be remembered clambered down the steep cliff, plunged into the boiling surf and succeeded in bringing the boat containing Hanson safely ashore. Hanson's companion, a boy named Ennion, was unfortunately drowned.

--oOo--

There were the three 'Dukes'. Duke of Lancaster, Duke of Argyll and Duke of Rothesay. When I come the Duke of Lancaster caught fire. It started one Friday night. They'd practically got the boat loaded. It tilted over and it caught the piles underneath of the boat ...

Duke of Lancaster, Heysham Harbour 1931
(It was refloated, restored and put back into service.)

Now, in the new Millennium, and after about a hundred years service, there have been many changes at the Harbour. The recent ones have all been for good. Ships to Belfast and the Isle of Man, roll-on-roll-off ferries, trade with many parts of the world, increasing expansion, Heysham Harbour has brought work to the area and increased its involvement with the community.

Reference
1. Klondyke is a region and Dawson a town in NW Canada, the scene of a world famous gold-rush in the years following 1896.

Heysham Peninsula
7. Living and making a living

Me daddy worked on the harbour when it was built.

He was a Pile driver. When that harbour was finished, he went to Immingham docks, at Grimsby, and he'd been somewhere at Fleetwood.

He finished that up and was just out of work when they got married. They got married on 30/-. They got married at Parish Church at St Peter's. Me daddy heard there was a job at Barton Bridge in Trafford Park, and he got a job there. He stuck it down there a bit and I was born there. Me daddy didn't like it down in Manchester and he got to know that Mr Stuttard (*the headmaster of the school*) knew of a house in the bottom at the back of the town before houses were pulled down. There were four houses back to back, two and two. He got to know one of them was empty. I was seven weeks old when they came back so it must have been February.

Old Rectory

Then they heard that Mrs Nicholson that was living in the Old Rectory was going to Canada. As soon as they heard they were going to Canada they let me daddy have the house. When he came back he was doing roads, new golf links, took the old golf links to where it is now. And we used to take his dinner on Long Lane, to Red Nab. We took a bottle of tea.

He wanted so much to be on his own. He started digging (worms?) and shrimping.

My first job was when I was 14. I left school at Christmas, and my first job was hawking fish. He - me daddy - went down to trawlers wi' tinnels - well I can make a tinnel - we call 'em tinnels instead of baskets. He went and bought some fish and then we had a spring balance, and he weighted 'em, maybe a pound or a pound and a bit, and put 'em all in sections with paper round 'em, and I used to go to the 'aristocracy' in Heysham. They lived in Eardley Road. Ever so posh. We did not think we were 'low-cast'.

Then I used to go on to Twemlow. We used to go on Seymour Grove, and they took pity on me and they said, 'Would you like a frock?'. I'd come back with a costume or a coat and stuff like that and they'd take an order for duck eggs. We used to sell duck eggs at ninepence a dozen and hen eggs at a shilling a dozen. When he was shrimping I'd get an order for some shrimps.

We had an allotment in Kirkgate. We used to grow strawberries, and grow lettuce. Then after that we started doing teas.

The tea garden

Me mother started with that tea garden. She brought the table out of the kitchen and two chairs, put it out in front ... Mother would make a few scones, bread and butter and boil an egg. People used to come and sometimes me mother would make a bit of jam and that's how we started. From two to four to six then seven.

No jobs in Heysham

There were no jobs in Heysham when I left school because you either had to go and be a maid and sit under other folks thumb and be a slave or you had to go to the bobbin mill and make bobbins.

Auction mart in Lancaster

If you wanted to go into farm service you had to go and stand at the auction mart in Lancaster. Hiring was at Martinmas. One of our relations did that. Me daddy used to go and see his old pals.

Ways and Means

When Mrs Taylor (daddy's Salvationist business associate) and me daddy didn't have much money, they bought a couple of potatoes, prayed about it and found two pounds. Mrs Taylor prayed about eggs and she got them.

---oOo---

Shop assistant

My job then was fruit and vegetables, general stores, eggs. I liked it.

Clogs

Before that I was in the shoe trade, clogs and other footwear. Mainly clogs. Nearly thirty years in Heysham. Woborrow Road. Everybody wore clogs in those days. Before Wellingtons came. That did it. Wellingtons killed the clog trade. I put irons on. In ten minutes. A full set would perhaps be threepence for a front iron and twopence for a heel iron. A pair of clogs for tenpence. It cost twelve and six for a pair of lace ones; the others didn't use as much leather and were cheaper. Shoe clogs cost nine or ten shillings. Children wore them - fancy ones with red uppers and with brass buckles.

---oOo---

Shrimping

We went shrimping. We've been down to the tide edge at two o'clock int' morning. Carried an arc lamp, and we had a labrador dog - and me daddy would go shrimping at tide edge from there right down to old lighthouse and then back again. When the tide was going out and when the tide was coming in. You know the harbour? The banking on this side before ever they built tankers, showing them to come into the harbour. We used to shrimp to there and then back again. We used to boil the shrimps in the middle of the night - or crabs. Crabs used to jump off the table when we were sorting them out. You know

Living and making a living

when the tide used to come in crabs used to come out. They were under the oil cloth or under the grandfather clock, but they knew when the tide was coming in.

Thunderstorms

I was terrified of thunderstorms If you were right out there and there was a thunderstorm, it was so frightening he used to say you'll be all right lass, and I used to run all the way home, and my mother, she used to go mad that I'd gone with him, but she knew he liked company.

Fishing in Heysham was done either on foot, wading down to the water, or with a pony and cart for shell fish, and also catching fish on nets, called baulks. Boats were not used generally. There were no fishing boats in Lower Heysham.

---oOo---

Peat Cutting

You know the nature reserve down Heysham Moss, where the peat beds are? Well, before I would say, middle eighteen hundreds, long before the railway line came through, it was the main source of burning material, peat. All Heysham used to go and cut it. Me father used to go and cut it. They used to stack it up until it dries you know. They used to cart the peat off ... there were only donkeys and small ponies in them days. No cars or wagons.

---oOo---

Coal Round

My father had a coal round, delivering in Morecambe and Heysham. Mrs Lister (of the Bradford Listers), every year around Christmas used to pay for a ton of coal. It had to be delivered in bags of a hundredweight to the people my father considered to be the poorest. It had to be delivered anonymously. If anyone enquired who the donor was they were not to receive the gift.

---oOo---

Gardening

I came from East Yorkshire. This head gardener - he was a welshman and he took the Gardeners' Journal. and it was full of places all over the country ... there was a place advertised at Heysham at White Lodge. People called Listers had it, Bradford wool people. Well, they made a big extension to the house. You know the Strawberry Gardens, there's Sugham Lane, well it was up Lister Grove. That's why they called it Lister Grove ... well, I got the job ... I was there three years ... and I went on the railway, in April 1935.

I joined up in 1940 and was away until the war finished. They had women working on the ships. Everything was moved by hand - two wheeled trucks - bales of bacon when I was there. Thirteen rolls of bacon in one lot, 4 to 4 and a half hundredweight.

Living and making a living

During the war they cut the size because women could not move 4 hundredweight.

---oOo---

Fishing in Overton

Apart from farming, there was fishing. Lune salmon and shrimps, shellfish. Boats were used. Some of the boats they use now must be over a hundred years old. There were four or five fishermen lived in Overton. The Braid family were mainly fishermen.

And Farming

We had a farm. It was either farming or fishing. Dad used to have one night a year away from home and he went to a sheep sale to buy sheep. We thought that was a great adventure - somewhere near Scotch Corner. The sheep used to come down on the train to Heysham Harbour and all the farmers would go there and bring them home. In those days it was all horse work. Tractors didn't come till after the war.

In those days there was no vet on call. My father used to be the local medicine man and was called out to sick animals. If I heard him getting up during the night, someone called him to check a cow calving, I'd get up and go with him. They'd come for him if a mare was in foal. If a farmer had a horse that wasn't behaving itself it would come to our farm for a week or two.

Changes

The Council built the new houses at Lancaster Road. One was designated for a farm worker. The rest of them worked at Heysham Harbour. The Harbour was one of the main employers. And of course the ICI during the war.

When I was a lad there were six farms in Overton. Now there are two. Four at Sunderland Point, now there is just one. Middleton about six. Middleton was ruined when the ICI came. They built the houses round the square. A few farms and cottages that's all there was at Middleton. Some of my relations lost their farms. Compulsorily purchased. Kicked them out. That was the sort of thing that happened.

There was a time when Mashiters and Baxters owned a lot of land round there. You can't see where the farms have been. Where the new pub is - the Crown and Anchor - was a farm. Roof Tree Inn, Uncle Billy Mashiter's farm house. We used to go there at Christmas and have a party. Auntie Bertha used to live there. We used to go past on the half-past eight bus (to the Grammar School in Morecambe), and they'd be getting their washing in. If they weren't getting their washing in as the half past eight bus went past, they were behind hand.

Living and making a living

Musseling at Heysham

More mussels are to be found on Heysham Skears than at any other place on the West coast. The skears are large tracts of rough ground, some parts of which are left uncovered by the ebb tide. The beds are not all productive at one time; they continually alter their position and their population, whilst the channels may shift and cover them with sand. In 1902-03 2000 tons of mussels were sent from these skears by rail.

(*Newspaper extract*)
Lancaster Castle : C T Royds presiding

Contrary to bye-laws.
Bailiff seized the rake. Mussels had to be scooped up with a rake when the mussels were covered with four feet of water. Mussels could be picked by hand when the mussels were on the sand. A fine of 10s was imposed, costs £1.10s. and the rakes were forfeited.

In 1874 the Lords of the Manor prosecuted the fishermen claiming ownership of these mussel beds and demanding rent. However, having confused ownership of fishing baulks with ownership of territory, they lost the case.

Heysham Peninsula
8. A Gardener's Diary

From 1st January 1884 to 10th July 1888 William Stephenson of Heysham kept a gardener's diary. Each day he describes the wind direction and other significant aspects of the weather. He was head gardener at Heysham Tower from before this time until his death in 1897. The house belonged to Mr Bennett who was probably in frail health at the time. Mr Bennett had sons living in Liverpool, to whom Mr Stephenson sent baskets of grapes and other fruit by rail, and baskets of flowers and grapes to hospitals and asylums and similar organisations locally.

Most plants and flowers are given their Latin names.

He worked every day except Sundays and Christmas Day.

These are some of his entries:

January 1884

Tuesday 1st : Wind south east, dull, fine. W. end Wind south east, dull, fine, began to dig the orchard, brought plants out of the Conservatory. Took others in. Cut down (wind) chrysanthemums.

Thursday 3rd : Wind south east moderate, drizzly rain all day. Working in the orchard. Pruned vines, potted plants.

Friday 11th : Wind north west stormy, heavy showers of hail. Digging in the orchard. Pruned vines in 2 (vinery). Repaired kitchen tap.

Thursday 17th : Wind south west moderate, dull, fair. Working in the orchard took the worm casts from the grass in the centre garden. Finished white-washing the new shed. Put fires in. Took R Woodmans planks home.

These kinds of entries make up the majority, but there are some interesting insights into local life.

On 3rd April he orders plants from Mr Shepston of Belper.

2 dozen wallflowers, Double yellow and dark
1 dozen Hollyhocks
4 dozen yellow Auriculas
2 dozen Alpines
Daisies.   6 hen and chickens
          6 Lady Hope
          6 White Queen
          6 Smiths White
          6 Flowers of Spring
          6 Early Red
          6 Defiance
2 Dozen Polyanthuses Mixed
2 Plants Harlequin
3 - do - Socratees
1 - do - Princess Thyru
1 - do - Isabela
1 - do - Lady Hardy
2 - do - Duchess de Morney

3rd (April) Wind south east moderate, fine, a shower. Cleaned walks. Washed bottles. Got in Hay. Planted Auriculas in Mr B's garden. Planted daisies, polyanthuses in north east garden. Potted hollyhocks, wallflowers, potted plants in No 8.

A Gardener's Diary

June 1885

18th ... R. Hodgson took out the horses for a drive.
19th ... R. Hodgson took the horses for a drive ...
and similarly on 20th, 22nd, 23rd, 24th, 25th, 26th, 27th, 29th, 30th; also on July 1st, 4th, 8th, 10th, 13th, 15th and 17th.
20th ... R. Hodgson took horses for a drive. Dr Saul brought 2 new horses to the Tower.
23rd ... Took the new horses back home.

September 1885

17th Wind south east moderate fine. Cleaned walks in south east garden. Mowed the grass by the drive. Destroyed 9 wasps nests. Mr B. died.
19th West strong showers. Put gravel on the top walk in centre garden. Put Mr B. into his coffin.
21st Wind north west moderate fine. Took Mr B. to Liverpool to inter.
Dec. 1st Wind west, moderate fine. Dug beds in south garden. Repaired the old rabbit house.
The first election under the New Franchise, Mr Marton, Capernraw (*sic*) and Mr MacCoan, Major Marton got the seat in parliament.

14th ... killed a pig by R. Hodgson.

Gardeners at Heysham Tower
William Stephenson, Head Gardener, is on the left.

15th ... Salted the pork.
16th ... Sent to Liverpool a Hamper of pork and apples.

April 1886

30th Wind east to west. Moderate fine frost. Ice half in thick. Cleaned the drive.

June 1888

25th ... Picked caterpillars from the gooseberry trees. Water peas and broccolis. Mrs Bennett died this afternoon between 4 and 5.

27th ... Cut flowers for wreathes and crosses.

28th ... Mrs B. interred.

The last entry incomplete because of a cut page, was on August 10th 1888.

Mr William Stephenson appears as gardener in the 1891 census and died at the age of 72 in 1897. He was head gardener at Heysham Tower. He and his wife lived in Tower Lodge with her son, Christopher Cornthwaite.

Mr Thomas Ogden, a visitor to the Tower spoke to him and in the middle of a sentence he suddenly fell with his face to the ground. He appeared to be dead a moment afterwards. The jury at the inquest agreed on a verdict of 'death by natural causes'.

Heysham Peninsula
9. Pastimes and Entertainment

Overton memories

We were a very close-knit community. We entertained ourselves. The treat of the year was the Sunday School trip. They used to take us to Blackpool. We used to have slide shows in the Chapel. Dances in the school. Live bands of course, no tape recorders. When I was 10 years old I used to play in a mouth organ band. That was in the school.

The annual treat in the village was the Sports Day. It was quite a big occasion. We used to have open sports and local sports. We had Cumberland and Westmorland wrestling in those days. The local lads would have a go but they couldn't compete with the regalia.

We used to play cricket. The village had an official team. There was more cricket in those days than football, nearly every village had a team. The cricket field was where this (Overton village hall) is now. We didn't play football.

Leaving the village was an event. Even Middleton was a foreign country, and Heysham and Morecambe was travelling abroad.

Outsiders came to give us a slide show. This was in the chapel. It would be filled. I went to both, chapel and church. I used to go four times on a Sunday. I sang in the choir, went to Sunday School.

The local preacher used to come from Morecambe. He'd come on the half past six bus, but he never caught the half past seven bus. The services went on for an hour and a quarter and he'd come to our house to wait. We'd sing round the piano. We'd sing hymns. My mother played. I don't know where she learned to play. She was not very self confident about it.

I used to have an uncle who played in a band that used to go round playing for dances. He came from Heysham. He was Wilbert Parker. He was a piano player.

--oOo--

The Heysham Club

Heysham had its own 'club', a sick club, raising money from the local families weekly, and paying out small sums in times of sickness, bereavement, or other adversity. It was also a social club for the men of the parish.

On the morning of New Year's Day all the male members of the club processed round the parish with banners accompanied by a brass band. This was followed by a church service, led by the Rector who was also the honorary chairman of the club. The annual accounts were discussed and a large dinner was held, either in the schoolroom or at the Royal Hotel, (depending on who did the catering), consisting of large quantities of roast beef and boiled mutton, enormous puddings and pies for sometimes a hundred and fifty men. Afterwards a large number of them went to the Royal Hotel and drank a large quantity of whatever the landlord could provide. Sometimes the women were invited in the evening for dancing, making it a social occasion.

Heysham Peninsula
10. Heysham Head

Childhood Memories

My thoughts on Heysham Head are it was good clean fun, a family place of enjoyment. You felt safe and free there, roaming about the woodland and also an access to the beach was provided with a man at the door who stamped your hand so you could get back in. The letters HH were stamped on the top of your hand in purple ink.

Travelling from the beach was quite a steep hill. Half way up was the Marionette Show. The kids loved it. My brother and I used to sit there and watch very intently. In fact all the kids sat very quietly watching the performance. They had the same routine every day. We knew it off by heart. Before the performance they sold programmes, and the lady with the blonde hair and glasses went round between the deck chairs. We used to mock this person as she had a rather squeaky voice. She would call out Yorkshire Bob in Fairyland at the top of her voice, and of course this amused the kids a lot.

On the programmes was a picture of Yorkshire Bob. He was the main theme for the show. There were two puppeteers, the husband and wife. She was the lady who sold the programmes. They had many puppets, which were all very different. A few I can recall were 'Pinky and Perky', Yorkshire Bob, a disjointing skeleton, and Punch and Judy.

Pinky and Perky

Travelling along about the same level was the children's playground. There was the big roundabout. We spun it round very fast and then jumped on. It must hold about twenty children, all with happy smiling faces. Nearby was the seesaw, only supposed to be two at a time, but sometimes we had four on the ride. Next came the old fashioned Swing Boats. There were four sets of six, and almost most of the time they were fully occupied. Sometimes we had to queue, as they always seemed to me the most popular ride. It was very exciting swinging very high. When you pulled on the rope you thought you were flying.

Further on still was the open-air dance floor facing the sea. At the former were four poles to which a big funnel loudspeaker was clipped, and the music was belted out for the dancers. It was very popular with the adults, and also the children dancing away.

Sometimes nearby they had sports events which I ran in, and also my brother. We

Heysham Head

practised and won many prizes. Usually it was about half-a-crown. That was a lot then to us kids. They had a Mother's race and my mother won many times. In fact we were a very competitive family, going up to Heysham Head almost every day in the school holidays.

Going further up the slope to the top of the hill was the cage of the Russian Brown Bear. We called him 'Teddy'. He walked up and down the cage. I liked him, but always thought he stank a lot.

My father was the village plumber and sometimes worked at Heysham Head on various jobs. Once he had to run a water pipe inside the bear's cage, and I don't think he was too pleased about working so near the bear. The pipe ran into a small tank so Teddy could take a bath. I have seen him rolling around in the water. Also there was a chain hanging from the top of the cage with an iron ball attached, and the bear played with it.

Going on from the bear through the arch doorway, turning left, were several mesh cages, one of which contained a peacock. He span his feathers out quite often, and I very much liked him. The colours of his plumage were beautiful alongside other birds and rabbits, doves, pigeons, budgies.

At the end of the cages which contained the birds was the slot machine arcade. You put in a penny, and the ball spun around. I was quite lucky and won several pennies. This suited me a lot and I got very excited. I can remember two more machines which were very old, in fact pre-Victorian. I used to put in a penny and there were pictures of ladies. I thought these were very naughty ladies undressing and bathing. They would be a great collector's item today.

Further on down some steps were more penny machines. There must have been about a hundred or so. One of my favourite machines was the Band machine. It contained a big drum, cymbals, brushes, trumpet and organ. It played loudly and you would think someone was in the machine playing it, but of course there wasn't. It was fully automated. I stood there and watched the performance many times. It was one of my favourite things in Heysham Head.

Going into the next room there were long distorting mirrors. Some made you look fat, others made you skinny and tall. There were made on the curve to make the distortion. I laughed at this. A lot of the kids made funny faces and made it funnier than ever.

Next came the parrots on stands. There were about six and we called out Pretty Polly, and sometimes they talked back. They were beautiful colours and there were two white ones. Coming out of the further entrance were all the rabbits in the hutches. There must have been about a dozen or so. They were grey, brown, black and white. The children liked these. Also, they sometimes let the rabbits out and they ran about wild and it was very difficult, I suppose, to get them back now I think about it, but didn't then.

Opposite the rabbit hutches was another dance floor. It was a replica of the other one. It was elevated about 14 ins so the rabbits ran underneath and had a great time. I can remember sliding on the dance floor and getting spells in my legs from ankle to thigh, and my mother used a needle to get these out every day for many days. I did scream as it hurt very badly. I learnt my lesson on the dance floor. I didn't do it again.

Coming down from the dance floor travelling along the gravel path you reached the Old Manor House. They used the front entrance for a tea room. You could get jugs of tea to take out for about two shillings. I remember the old paved floor inside.

Many people from the Village worked in Heysham Head. It was a good source of employment.

From the Manor House down the wide steps with iron ornamental flower troughs either side was the Rose Garden where Concert parties were held. Bands from Yorkshire and Lancashire played on Sunday afternoons. My grandfather went every Sunday, with his best suit on and a carnation, which he grew himself, in his buttonhole. The Concert Party was on every day. There were singers. One I recall was Pat, a young girl about fourteen. She could sing and dance and play the accordion. She was very talented, and a good personality. She wore a lovely pink checked dress with a bow in her hair. Her father and mother were singers too and played the accordion and piano.

Part of the Rose Garden at Heysham Head
(from a 1933 holiday brochure)

Heysham Head

There was another act called 'Windy Lyle'. She was a ventriloquist dressed in an RAF uniform. The dummy was too. Also there was a clairvoyant who was blindfolded on stage, and her accomplice went around the audience getting articles off the public and she would identify them. I never did fathom how they did it, being a child at the time.

Uncle Bill Mann was another entertainer. He used to whistle to the tune 'If I were a Blackbird'. Also he ran the Children's Talent competition at 5 o'clock every evening, in which my brother and I sang at various times. The competition was very strong. I recall a boy with a voice like angel, like a choir-boy, singing 'Jerusalem' at the top of his voice. He also had a caliper on his leg. He won every time. He stole the show. It was so moving to hear such a voice clear as a bell singing such a song. The adults were in tears.

A bit more about the Rose garden itself. It was very beautiful. Roses everywhere. Apple trees were growing up the side of the walls with blossom in spring. There were alcoves with seating from which you could watch the concert. There were wooden chairs and benches throughout the area. There were several statues and sculptured pots of original design, which all added to the Victorian atmosphere of the beautiful garden. What a gem.

Above the Rose garden up the hill was the circus. It had two performances a day. It was run by 'Gandys'; a family concern. On show was a black pony. It had five legs. I have never seen anything like it since.

In the show were clowns, horses, dogs, trapeze acts, tightrope walkers, magicians, and sometimes they had children to join in the fun.

Another family-run circus was the one by the 'Ross' family, and at this present time a member of the family still resides in the area.

Over the years, people still ask about Heysham Head. They have told their children, and now their grandchildren, about it, and they are more curious than ever about what went on in those days. The thing is you could afford to spend a whole day up there with children, and it would not cost the earth. I think it was about sixpence each, and once up there everything was free, other than food or drinks. It is a great pity we have lost such a venue as this. It was irreplaceable and a great loss to the town as a whole.

Heysham Peninsula
11. Some Heysham buildings

The Ancient Water Mill

Stephen de Moleyns of the stock represented by Lord Sefton, bought the mill in Higher Heysham in the 13th century, where his son made famous bows and arrows marked 'The Grange' and also mended armour and jewellery. Afterwards a dam was constructed across the little brook which ran down the dell where Middleton Road now is, and a water mill giving increased power became famous. The bows were made of yew and the arrows of ash. The son, Thomas de Moleyns, was educated at the Priory of St Mary, Lancaster, and he used to draw up legal documents for people in the district.

Carr Garth : The Old School
(Bailey Lane)

The main part of the building facing NNE is reported to date from the 1600s. The exact year is not known, as the original deeds to the property have long since been lost.

The building attached to the rear of the house is, however, said to be much older, possibly a hundred years or more, bringing it into the 1500s.

Not a lot of information has been discovered about the building by Ann and Brian Patterson who owned the building until recently, but, in the early 1800s,

Carr Garth, Bailey Lane

Heysham buildings

perhaps about 1840 it became a school, which it remained until possibly 1900.

In the Heysham Directory for 1851 on p. 529, it states that there are two schools in the Village. One the Parish School, run by the Church, the other 'Carr Garth', which it states was built (*possibly meaning 'Renovated and Extended'*) and supported by John Knowlys Esq, of Heysham Tower, who, on the 8th October 1850, died from the effects of a pistol shot.

The first Headmaster of the School was a Mr James Mashiter, who came from South Lancashire. His niece kept house for him. So far nobody seems to be able to trace any school Records or documents etc, but apparently in its days as a school it had a very good name. Many people who became well known upholders of society, were educated there. One of the most famous was James Williamson who later became Lord Ashton of Lancaster. To this day his initials and date, J.W. 1854 can be found scratched on the kitchen window which may have been a classroom at that time.

During the first World War (1914-1918) Carr Garth was used as a convalescent home for officers. It was offered for this purpose by the then owner, a Miss Smith in 1915, who said that it had to be used as 'a Convalescent Home for our brave troops for the duration of the War'.

In 1920 the property was taken over by the church and made into a guest house for the clergy. During this period, the old school bell was removed from the roof at the rear of the building. Apparently it took three days before they managed to lower it down to the ground.

In 1950 the property was purchased by Norman and Alice Walkington, the parents of the recent owners. The Walkingtons continued to run the place as a guest house until 1970, when they handed it over to their daughter and son-in-law who continued to run it as a guest house. (*The Pattersons sold the house in 1995*).

The name Carr Garth is of Norse origin. Carr or Scarr, meaning a jagged or precipitous rock or sea cliff, and Garth, meaning enclosed area or paddock. *(There is a quarry immediately behind the building.)*

Mr Knowlys was said to be critical of the local school as 'not evangelical enough', hence the reasons for starting the new school. The schoolmaster was not related to the local Mashiters who at this time were farmers.

Heysham Bobbin Mill.
(Trumacar Side)

It is curious sequence of fact that almost on the site of the Ancient Water Mill which made renowned arrows and long bows in the 13th century, there should arise another factory in 1908 which made the finest wooden bobbins for the textile industry. Wilkinson & Sons employed 60 - 70 people. The bobbins were made of beech and birch, but for the linen industry were made out of teak, because of its waterproof qualities.

The Battery
(This account was written some 40 years ago.)

From 1867 to 1876, and of course long before any promenade was made at the West End, the Battery site was being used as an artillery range. The position occupied the site of the present Battery Inn Extension the Palace Theatre and the Parking Ground across Sefton Road (*no road then*). There were remains of a few cottages at the rear of the Battery and to the right rear was the Old Windmill Round House (*see Mill House near the top of the map on p. ii*), used as a side arms stand locker - a store for fuses and shell implements. The magazine was to the left back of the house. The officers and instructors also used it for a shelter. This Battery site was used by the 7th & 8th Batteries of the 29th Lancashire Artillery Volunteers.

There was a great storm in 1876 undermining the platforms, also the increasing danger of steamers and strangers in boats being hit by the projectiles, and the constant removal of shingle and sand from the point, caused the removal of the Battery to Bare, the last position being at Scalestones Point.

The Old Hall, Heysham
(Middleton Road)

Originally built in 1598 it was first occupied by three tenants. The Manor of Heysham belonged to Lord Monteagle, who sold it to John Bradley of Chipping who died the same year, leaving the estate to his daughter Jane, wife of John Leyburne. The house was occupied by tenants, the first being Robert Edmondson. It has been presumed that Robert was elevated to steward by the Leyburnes and given the means to build the house which would otherwise have been out of his reach. At the time it was the largest in the parish. The Leyburnes were devout Roman Catholics and the house may have been some sort of reward for Robert's loyalty. There were once secret passages 'Priest's holes' for hiding illegal priests. In 1607 Robert was described as a 'poor Popish recusant unable to pay 8d fine'.

Mr Richard Caton bought the hall in 1807; it was then known as 'Wren Hall' or 'Heysham Hall'.

The next owner traced was Rev John Royds who bought the property in 1857. The Hall was occupied by members of the Royds family until sometime before 1956 when the property was sold to Wm. Barker, a brewer of Lancaster.

The last occupant of the Hall as a private house was the Rector's sister, Miss Maggie, who towards the end of her life was something of a recluse.

Heysham buildings

The Old Hall, Heysham

Unfortunately the house almost fell into dereliction until it was saved by the brewer and turned into a fine inn.

The Old Rectory - Greese Cottage (Main Street)

Tradition has it that the house was built by William Ward, Rector of the Parish at the time of the date stone. This may or may not have been the case. There is an earlier carving of the date inside the house on a beam which makes the house much earlier than would appear. However, it is always possible that the house was not called the Rectory until the Clarkson family of rectors came in 1735. The Clarkson family were consecutive rectors of Heysham for about a hundred years - Rev Robert Clarkson taking over on the death of his father or grandfather.

It is unlikely to have been used by T D Whitaker in 1814 as he made unflattering remarks about the 'Parsonage House' on the south side of the church.

The Laytham family occupied the house from about 1916, when the family came from Manchester. The father, Bill, worked on a casual basis for the Royds family, and he was said to be a fine shot. He was a great favourite with Everard Royds, who was one of the last curates of the Royds family to serve in Heysham.

Heysham Peninsula
12. History beneath my feet

When all the land around a small village - like Heysham, for example - is built upon, and the fascia and interior of the older buildings have been altered beyond recognition, most people think that their heritage and history have gone forever.

This is far, far, from the truth. In fact, the real search for your Village history has only just begun.

Anyone who has had a family in the Village for two or three generations, will have in their possession: old photographs, post-cards, letters, deeds, and perhaps an old tithe map of the parish - showing the amount of money or produce to be paid annually to the church or Village manor. This is one part of your history still available for your research.

To me, the main part of my research is what I find beneath my feet.

For over thirty years now I have been out and about in Heysham Village and surrounding areas with my metal detector (with the permission of the landowners), and in that time I have found hundreds of metal artefacts. These items were of no value to the farmers/landowners, but were of great historical value to me. I have found coins and trade weights from the Roman period, coins, loom weights, spindle whorls

Elizabeth I
Sixpence 1569

Elizabeth I
Threepence 1569

Henry VII Silver Penny
(Sovereign Type : York mint.
Archbishop Rotherham
keys below shield

- 51 -

History beneath my feet

and buckles from the Anglo-Saxon period, silver coins, buckles, crotal bells (cow-bells) and pilgrim's ampullas from Mediaeval times. There are coins, buckles, cloak fasteners from the Tudor period, and coins, military badges and jewellery from the 19th and 20th centuries.

All these, when placed in their proper time context, show a continuous occupation of our area throughout every period of history.

(*Anyone reading this who wishes to get into the hobby of metal detecting, please contact Tony Ross at St Peter's C of E School.*)

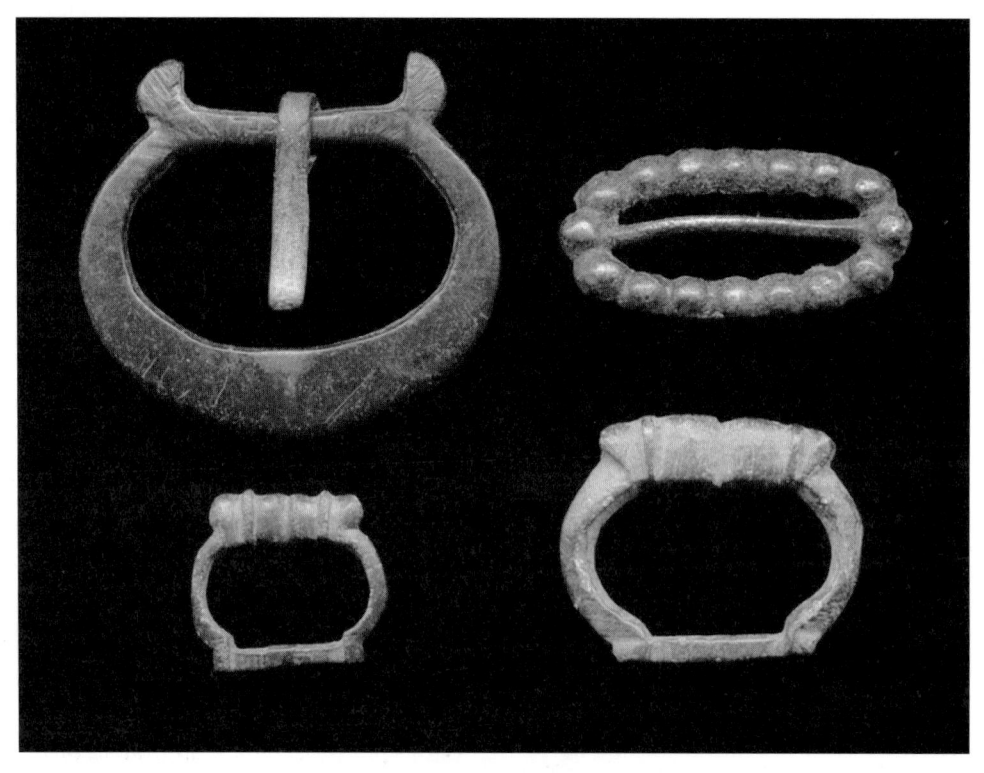

Very early bronze buckles

Heysham Peninsula
13. Education

[*St Peter's School, Heysham, as we now know it, was known during the 19th century as a 'National School' under the National Society, founded by the Church of England in 1817; the school predates the Society. Board Schools came into being following the Forster Education Act of 1870.*]

Recorded in the Heysham registers of Births, Burials and Marriages is a 'Copy of Foundation Plate of Heysham School'.

This School was Erected Anno Dom. 1769 at the sole expense of those whose Name and Subscriptions are hereon engraved, upon a Piece of Ground for which an Annual Rent of Eighteenpence is to be paid by the Schoolmaster, for the time being to the Rev Mr Clarkson, the present Rector and to his Successors, Rectors of Heysham, for ever.

There follows a list of 25 Subscribers whose donations vary from £9.0.0. (*from the Rector*) to 1.0 (*one shilling*) from Marg. Padget. These subscribers set out Rules and Orders for the Management of 'this School and the Conduct of the said Schoolmaster'.

That every Person or Persons of Property within the said Parish of 10 L (£10) per Anno or upwards, who has not already subscribed to the said School or their Tenants shall pay One Shilling p. Quarter for every Scholar sent by him or them over and above the Subscribers Quarterly Pay.

That the Schoolmaster and every succeeding Master make or cause to be made good all windows that shall be broke by any of his Scholar or Scholars.

That he teach the Scholars or hear them repeat the Church Catechism once every week.

That he attend the School in the Summer Season, viz from the 25th of March to the 29th September from 7 o'clock to 12 o'clock in the forenoon and from 2 to 5 o'clock in the afternoon.

In the Winter, viz. from the 29th Sep. to the 25th March, that he attend from 8 to 12 o'clock in the forenoon and in the afternoon from 1 to 4 o'clock.

The above agreed by a Majority of the Subscribers in number and value the 5th May 1779, who caused this to be engraved and fixed up the sd. School.

A further document, an Indenture deposited at the Public Records Office dated 19th June 1817 between Robert Thompson of Cheetwood, Manchester and Robert Mashiter and Robert Banks both of Heysham (*Churchwardens*) in which Robert Thompson gives to the others the sum of one hundred pounds

... 5 per cent consolidated annuities ... In trust to dispose of the same on the education of eight poor Girls belonging to the parish of Heysham ... to augment the said Charity and to establish the same for ever for the education and instruction poor children both boys and girls belonging to the said parish in the principles of the Church of England ...

Education

provide useful learning for poor children, that is to say the Boys to read write and to cast accounts and the Girls to read write knit and work plain work and all the said children, both boys and girls to be educated and instructed in the principles of the Church of England as by law established and to read and say their Catechism and upon further Trust that the children to be admitted to the said charity shall one half of them be ... chosen in Easter week in every year and shall be continued for the term of two years, so that one half of the whole number to be instructed as aforesaid shall be elected and chosen and one half retire at the feast of Easter in every year and that such a number shall be from time to time instructed as the funds of the said charity will be sufficient to support ... the said poor children during the time they are receiving the benefit of the said charity shall go in procession to the parish church at Heysham aforesaid ... on every Sunday to hear divine service ... and that for their more orderly appearance they go two and two the girls first and the Boys to follow each two to go at the distance of about five or six feet from the two who follow ...

The Education Act of 1870 made education available for all, but it was not until 1880 that education became compulsory.

Extracts from the School Log Book: February 2nd 1877 to June 20th 1896.

I was obliged to send the Parkinsons home today for their money.

February 12th : The attendance is very small this morning owing to anniversary of a Northern custom called 'Hard Graining'.

April 6th : Miss Bennett visited this morning and gave the children some sweets.

May 18th : Several of the children are engaged at their homes with the spring cleaning. Gave the school holiday until Wednesday - being Whitsuntide.

July 24th : Most of the children supplied themselves with exercise and copy books.

August 13th : Arthur Stuttard took charge of Heysham National School this day.

September 14th ... Miss Grafton, Heysham Hall, visited the school this day and heard the children sing.

October 9th : The children left the school shortly after 4 o'clock for the purpose of receiving a treat from the family of F.W.Grafton Esq. of Heysham Hall.

Oct 15th : ... Annie Burrow swallowed a small marble during playtime this afternoon.
... W Bennett Esq Heysham Tower visited the school today.

November 23rd : I have begun to collect the money for the fire. The children each bring threepence before and the like sum after Xmas to defray the cost of fuel.

November 30th : Mrs Ward resumed her duties (*sewing teacher*). In drying one of the school registers before the fire Mrs Ward's daughter scorched it.

Education

1878 February 4th : I have had to punish several of the elder boys for annoying the little ones in the playground and for taking their marbles.

September 3rd : The attendance not very good this week in consequence of the farmers being at the Agricultural show, and the children being kept to look after the houses.
The amount received for school fees during the past two weeks has been very large, 28/7d each week.

October 18th : All the first class of boys was away from school in the afternoon perambulating the boundaries of the manor of Heysham.

1880 January 8th : There is holiday today and tomorrow in consequence of the annual dinner to the Sunday scholars.

January 9th : No school because it could not be got ready after the dinner.

April 9th ... Many of the children have to go to the skeer.

September 1st : Holiday in consequence of choir treat.

September 3rd : Holiday in consequence of the Children's treat.

1883 March 14th : The attendance for this week is the best for nearly twelve months. During two quarters of the year whooping cough was very prevalent, and during the last summer several farmers went to Manitoba taking their families with them.

1884 September 4 : A great falling off in the attendance, caused by children being gathering blackberries.

September 11th Many children still away. On inquiry last week I was informed that a child could gather a dozen and a half quarts (*of blackberries*) in the week, and that Morecambe affords a ready market at prices from 4 pence to sixpence per quart.

1886 October 27th : Holiday in consequence of choir trip to Liverpool.

1888 April 12th : The Rev C T Royds visited the school. He informed me that it would be desirable to withdraw Thomas Woodman from active work as he is suffering from St Vitus' dance.

1890 November 5th : Miss Cawthra, Heysham Tower, called and invited the children to a bonfire and firework display this evening.

November 28th : The attendance is improving, but whooping cough has not wholly disappeared.

December 12th : Several children are again away, attacks of whooping cough having returned.

1891 October 12th : In consequence of information that Mary Outhwaite, Margt. Outhwaite, Wm. Hodgson, and Eliza Hodgson were suffering from itch, I directed Mr Stuttard to request their parents to keep them from school until they should be free from the disease.
                                    C Twemlow Royds

Education

1892 August 25th : School closed on Thursday afternoon and all day on Friday that the parents of children might attend garden party at the Rectory to meet Mr & Mrs Otley (Miss Lily Royds). Children's treat on Friday.

1894 September 11th : School closed on account of Friendly Society Jubilee.

1895 October 25th : School closed in the afternoon to enable younger children to have a treat provided at the strawberry gardens by Mrs J Royds.

1896 June 20th : Half holiday in consequence of some of the children being away at a picnic.

July 17th : The attendance this week is rather better. The registers were marked and closed at 1.30 so that children might go home at 3.30. During the Morecambe season many children are wanted on Friday afternoon to carry visitors' luggage or errands.

September 16th : Half holiday on account of cricket match.

September 25th : Half holiday in consequence of a Harvest Home at Overton.

December 2nd : The Heysham Golf Club require a number of boys as 'caddies' and the parents of boys have asked to allow them to go. I have therefore decided to mark and finally close the registers for morning school at 9.30 and for afternoon school at 11.35. The lessons will be as shown on time-table etc. 4 lessons of 25 minutes each. Ten minutes will be allowed for lunch and ordinary recreation.

This arrangement is temporary and only for Wednesdays.

I have discovered that the above arrangement is contrary to the code. It is therefore abandoned.

December 16th : Half holiday that boys may go to golf links.

1897 July 6th : Holiday on account of marriage of Mr J F T Royds.

July 7th : The attendance on Wednesday afternoons is very bad, most of the boys going to the golf links to act as caddies. I have called the attention of the school attendance officer to the matter, and he has promised to attend to it.

Many changes

Mr Arthur Stuttard was appointed in August 1877. He was head at Heysham until 1915. He ran the school with one teacher, Mrs Ward (infants and sewing, widow of the previous head master), even though the numbers on his register were excessive by any standards. The numbers varied between 133 and 96 up to the time of the invasion by the children of navvies in 1898. All during his stay at Heysham he was troubled with overcrowding, and with the advent of Klondyke and Dawson City this became much worse.

New children

At the beginning of 1898 the newly built huts were being occupied by the families.

Education

The first children came from Dawson City on February 14th 1898. These huts had been built for the 'skilled' men and at first were regarded as better class. Shortly after their arrival the school was closed due to an epidemic of whooping cough.

Then there was a rebellion by the local families. The school log book says:

> April 18th, 1898 : Considerable numbers of new scholars admitted chiefly from huts of Railway Company. Several children withdrawn from school, on the ground that parents do not like their children associated with navvies.

By November the same year there had been over a hundred new admissions. Some would have been from the native families of Heysham, but the local names and addresses could have been counted on one hand. Still they continued to arrive. Whilst numbers in the following years did not quite match this first influx, between February 1898 and March 1903 when the numbers really began to subside, 400 pupils with Klondyke or Dawson City addresses had passed through the school at Heysham.

Some did not stay long, some stayed and settled in the area. The records are erratic. The Master did not always enter the date of a child leaving the school and rarely did he give a reason for leaving. Some children stayed two years, others varied between one month and thirteen months. There was a lot of absenteeism and regular visits by the attendance officer - shared with the National schools and Board schools in Morecambe - had little or no effect, and attendance was sporadic.

School Visits

The sub-inspector I H Park visited the school on 28th September 1898.

> The deficiency of staff noted at the Examination still continues and the earliest possible action should be taken to remedy it for it is undoubtedly a serious matter that a teacher qualified only for 30 children should for a long period be taking 60 and upwards. The little girl now helping of course does not count on the effective staff. There also continues to be an inadequate supply of suitable desks ...

> The Headmaster had himself 56 in Standards IV - VI so that he is fully occupied and that under crowded conditions as regards II and III so that he cannot afford any relief.

The weather contributed to attendance figures:

> The weather has been bad again this week, and prevents children from the outlying districts coming regularly to school. Although there have been 142 children present during the week, the average is only 105 ...

Visit without notice

27th June 1899. Visit by J S Forster.

> The school is overcrowded in both of the rooms. This morning the Infant Boys

Education

were in the playground for a writing lesson, kneeling on the ground, with benches for desks.

The staff does not satisfy the requirements of Article 73.

Mr Stuttard announced that:

A school has been opened in the Navvy Mission room at Klondyke by the Missionary's daughters. The Summary this week shows that the number of children on the books at this school is 148 of whom 134 have been in actual attendance.

G E Stuttard (daughter of Arthur Stuttard) is recognised under Article 33. Miss Moxon is continued under Article 68.

Occasionally the school had to be closed due to the absence of the Master. This also happened if there was a fall of snow, and when the weather was wet the children were often sent home.

> March 9th 1900 : The Rev C T Royds, Manager of this school, died suddenly this day. He will be very much regretted by all connected with the school. In him, the teachers especially, have lost a kind and courteous friend.

The slight easing of numbers created by the Navvy Mission school did not last long, By March 1900 the average of 133 for the week drew the comment 'It is mainly impossible to run the school in such large numbers'. Three days later a grant was received for the 'improvement of staff - an additional probationer at £11.0.0. per annum'.

And yet again there is sudden surge in the school population.

> School is disrupted whilst building work took place, children dismissed early so that the workmen could begin.

> August 3rd : School closed for Midsummer holidays (4 weeks). The attendance has not been good during the last week. Many children are engaged in getting up potatoes and some are wanted for carrying luggage, etc.

Although from 1870 Education had been available for all, many of the children of school age had not been to school before. Whether this was deliberate or by default we shall never know; whether it was because families moved about a lot, or whether it was because they did not regard education as important, we have no knowledge.

1901 Miss Hanna Butler, Infants School, Settle, commenced duty.

> February 1st : The new quarter shows there are 191 scholars on the registers but only 171 have been attendance this week.

The places they came from give no clue to this. This is no apparent consistency in the places they came from immediately before Heysham. A large number came from places where there were harbours - Barry, Grimsby, Hull, Fraserburgh, or from

Education

railway towns such as Knottingley, Carnforth and Warrington, but there were others from the industrial towns of mid-Lancashire, Manchester, Bolton, and there was almost an invasion from Yorkshire - Leeds, Birstall, Bruntcliffe, Brighouse, Bingley and Sheffield. There were also people from less likely areas such as Pateley Bridge, Hutton Roof and St Annes.

The children may not all have been the sons and daughters of navvies, but if they lived in the huts at Klondyke and Dawson City we have to assume that their fathers worked in some capacity at the harbour.

March 29th : Master will be absent on Monday in connection with census.

June 2nd : The Rector desired that the children should have a holiday on the proclamation of Peace. (*End of the South African Boer War*)

Setting the Standard

Faced with children at many stages of education, or without it completely, it was some time before Mr Stuttard was able to present them in a 'Standard' (rather like the current National Curriculum Tests).

In 1903 he recorded that he presented a large number in Standard II.

These children were between the ages of 9 and 14, but should have been 7 plus. After this some notice was taken of the Standard reached at a child's previous school, but it was rarely higher than Standard II regardless of the age of the child. In only one case was Standard VI reached, and that by James Kerr, from Glasgow, a twelve-year old who had reached Standard V before coming to Heysham. According the results and the amount of criticism received from visiting HMIs, the quality of education was below the average, which was not surprising considering the disadvantages of the school.

June 29th : Owing to a serious outbreak of small-pox among the people at Klondyke, the Managers have given orders that children from that district have not to be admitted. From this department 30 children have been excluded. (*Vaccination had been compulsory from 1853.*)

School Board.

On December 4th 1900 the Morecambe Visitor had a long editorial, entitled 'Voluntary versus compulsory'. In it the writer attacked the stand made by the church against a School Board with the alternative of another National School. Until this time the church had controlled local education absolutely, and was accused of providing education that was not sufficient for these progressive times.

Mr Stuttard was present at a vestry meeting in which the matter was discussed

Education

He knew what salaries were and the cost of educating children, and it was probably the economics that were the deciding factor, but it was only by a narrow margin of 21 for to 19 against that a motion was passed in favour of a Board School.

At a later public meeting on February 25th the school was closed to decide by election whether Heysham should have a Board School. The result of this election was For 186, Against 104.

6th November, The Visitor
Heysham School Board

Discussion of the attendance at the two schools ... Employment of children scouring the district for absentees. This had happened in Morecambe some little time back, but Morecambe had put their foot down. A school attendance officer is employed, and parents will have legitimate cause for complaint if children are sent out to do his work.

The School opened in September of that year in the Wesleyan Schoolroom.

> Opened school at 9 am when 103 scholars attended.

It was not until August 29th 1904 that the new school, now called Sandylands, was opened in a newly erected building and the Wesleyan Methodist premises vacated.

There were two staff, Mr McGregor, the Headmaster, and Miss Emily A Marshall, assisted by a probationer, Miss G Topham, '... until additional assistant appointed'. Miss Nellie Walsh was appointed on October 23rd.

On the whole the staffing problems were far less than those of Mr Stuttard at the National School, but as with that school the number of children on roll continued to grow.

On the day Sandylands opened Mr. Stuttard reported:

> ... Resumed school. The approaching completion of the Harbour Works has somewhat thinned the school.

He must have been very thankful. For the first time the HMIs visiting the school are praising his work and the work of his staff, and the realisation has come that Klondyke and the harbour workers are not likely to be a permanent feature of the area.

Heysham Peninsula
14. Storms

5th February 1913
Morecambe Visitor

Referring to Mr Wilson recalls an old story of his bravery in rescuing the people from the old 'Pot-houses', which stood on the shore a little further seaward than Mr. John Hatch's present house, and which were then washed away in a great storm. A few still remember his going into the houses with the sea coming through them and bringing Mrs Calvert ashore, returning again to fetch some of her belongings which she was greatly distressed at having left behind. As he went in the second time a feeling ran through the watchers that he would not come out again, but he did, with a bag over his shoulder containing the papers and cash-box which he had ventured back for.

It is difficult to fix the exact date of this storm, but it would be about 1851. Christmas Day was on a Saturday and the storm was on the following Monday.

Building the Harbour

As with most coastal areas Heysham was very much at the mercy of the weather, especially the wind. An anemometer registered 100mph at Heysham in 1903. From the very beginning of the operation precautions had to be taken to ensure that the work done was not undone by the wind and tides.

In constructing the embankments a trench was first cut in the sand and filled with sandstone rock to form a toe and to prevent erosion by the sea. Provision had also to be made for protecting these tips during stormy weather by keeping in reserve a set of wagons filled with stone.

At least once during the construction the wagons were pushed off the site and into the sea to reduce encroachment.

Written about 1950

Opposite the entrance to the harbour are the steel masts and wire stays of a wreck whose hull is now buried in the sand. This was the steamer 'Western Valley', registered out of Swansea. She was bound from Port Briera to Heysham with Spanish Iron ore, and on the night of December 31st 1924 was anchored outside the harbour. A gale caused the anchors to drag and she went aground where she now is. A Heysham native was on board, and the crew took to the boats and landed close to the North breakwater. The wreck is now used as a drying place for cormorants.

An eyewitness account

FD's father died in 1921 in the 'flu epidemic after the war. Quite a lot of them died. And they buried him in the middle of the churchyard. Well not quite in the middle. He was buried where they put that new wall at the bottom and the

Storms

Bay Cottage (Pot House), Heysham Village Bay

tide came in and washed it all out in 1927 when there was a great storm, and it came over and washed the coffin out of a child, or it may have been two children, and the coffin was washed up at the Pothouse. Parson Royds, he went up and put his gown on and fetched the coffin to be buried again. Before the police came to keep you away - because when they got word we had to stay away - well, we went there and we saw his toes. All his toe nails, all good and just a bit of bone and stuff on and that. And I said well anybody who has been dead ten years their toe nails are as good as new. They were telling us not to go, but I went, and it was really frightening.

Heysham Peninsula
15. Heysham Village Institute

To: Heysham Parish Meeting.
From: Rev C T Royds, June 14 1897.

I have however the pleasure to repeat the offer made in my letter of the 3rd inst. to the Parish Council, the Property which I will hand over as a gift to the Parish on the occasion of the Queen's Diamond Jubilee is situated on what is known as the Square & consists at present of a barn & coach-house & two stables. This is room on the site for what is required & the Freehold with the Building Material on at the service of the parish. As the matter may require some little consideration I will keep the offer open for a couple of months from this date should the result be the establishment of a Library & Reading room. I trust that under good management it may conduce to the welfare & happiness of the parishioners.

I am Mr Chairman & Gentlemen,
Very Faithfully Yours,

Twemlow Royds

Although the site and buildings were a gift, money still had to be raised for its conversion and equipment, so a committee was appointed to try and raise the funds.

By today's standards the funds necessary seem small. Where men worked for an employer wages were low. At this time it would not be unusual for a workman to earn about 10 shillings a week

Most of the men in the village were small farmers, gardeners, agricultural workers or employed by the few better off as general labourers.

Although wages were low we must not assume that they would be regarded as 'poor'. They were self-sufficient in the food they grew and 'swapped'. There was always fish and shell-fish to be had. Most people had an allotment, kept chickens and ducks and a pig, which could supplement an otherwise small income.

The first committee consisted of members of the Parish Council with the power to add.

Some of the names of the first committee members will be familiar: Mashiter, Casson, Sandham, Tomlinson, Dowthwaite, and in the early stages Mr Stuttard, the schoolmaster, was on the committee.

They produced circulars asking for donations, and members were nominated to go out and collect on a regular basis, pennies or tuppences a week. By August 1897 the collections had brought in a massive total of eighty-five pounds.

The Institute had many supporters. The Heysham Cab Proprietors handed over the proceeds of 'drives', which amounted to £5 11s 6d after expenses had been deducted.

At this time the meetings were still being held in the National School room (now St Peter's School).

Heysham Village Institute

Land was purchased from Mr N Blacow at the back of the Institute. Plans were drawn up by Messrs Thompson & Parkinson, Architects. The price for the mason work was £89 5s 0d, and the joiner work £69 10s 0d. Mr John Clark's offer to cart so many stones from Mr Smalley's quarry, the stone to be carted gratis as a subscription was accepted with thanks.

With the completion of the Institute, the committee could now set up a scale of charges.

> Political Meetings : £1 5s 0d
> County Council :   £1 0s 0d
> Outside the district 15/- , Piano 2/6 extra
> Village Parties 10/- , Piano 2/6 extra
> Religious Meetings & District Council Meetings 5/-
> Reading Room 5/-

In December 1902 it was decided to buy a billiard table and local dignitaries were asked for their support. Money was raised with a 'draw' : tickets at 3d each. The secretary was instructed to buy a walking stick as a special prize for the draw. The winning numbers would be published in the Lancashire Daily Post.

Concerts were arranged. Meat & potato pie suppers, whist drives, were organised to raise money for the billiard table. Gas fittings and pendant were also needed. (*Unfortunately they forgot to minute the cost of the table!*)

It would cost a 2d for a game of billiards for 20 minutes, and it was set down what the score should be and the time allowed. The 20 minute rule for Billiards had to be enforced. Two weeks later it was unanimously agreed to buy a clock!

In November 1906 it was decided to purchase a Punch Ball and other games.

During this time the Royds family continued to support the Institute. Mr Royds used the Reading Room on Sundays. Mrs Royds organised concerts. In 1913 after one of these concerts concern was expressed as to the conduct of juniors, and it was agreed that for the future a special small committee be appointed to supervise all gatherings in connection with the Institute. (*Whatever were they doing?*)

There was also a Heysham Debating Society. Capt Bates Esq gave a paper. Subject: 'Should the Volunteer Force be disbanded and conscription be made compulsory?'. This was in 1913.
(*Was the Society overtaken by events in 1914?*)

The Institute was first and foremost a Reading Room, but rarely was reading mentioned. However it must have been a place where regular members could read the daily papers, because it was agreed to add the following to the Newspaper list. Wide Wide World Magazine, Pearson Weekly and the Royal Magazine.

The second World War brought the Institute into fighting mode. Fire Watching took place during the blackout, and fire equipment was obtained. The secretary purchased a stirrup pump and three buckets. Several villagers were in the Home Guard and ARP, and others on duty at the Harbour late at night.

As many of the members had left to join up boys were allowed to join the membership; there were complaints about their bad language, and occasionally one was suspended.

The Womens Volunteer Service ran a canteen. The room was let for concerts and community singing, but not on Sundays.

Towards the end of the war there was an influx of evacuees, presumably escaping from the London flying bombs. The Institute was used as a school room.

In March 1947 the weighing machine, abandoned at the outbreak of war, was sold to Avery's Ltd for £5.

J Edmondson asked permission for a weighing machine to be placed in front of the Institute for a rental of £12 for the season. The committee asked for rental in advance.

At a Public Meeting in November 1951 the finances of the Institute led to the possibility of closure. Mr Cropper suggested a committee of equal numbers of men and women, which was passed.

Before the following Annual General Meeting the minute was rescinded and the Institute returned to the status quo. It is only in recent years that the Institute has decided to accept women as members.

Heysham Peninsula
16. Overton

Some historians believe that Overton has a connection with the Romans, but so far no evidence for this has been produced. However it is an historic village, mentioned in the Domesday book as Oureton. The acreage of land was four carucates - a carucate being as much land as could be ploughed in a year by eight oxen with one plough.

The Manor of Overton was held at various times by John o'Gaunt and Sir John Lawrence. The Vicar of Lancaster received the tithes. Farmers paid in kind for the use of the Duke's mill to grind their corn. The Prior of Lancaster had a grange (a storage barn) in Overton in 1272.

The oldest building is the church. Originally dedicated to St Patrick, it was rebuilt in 1140 in Norman style. It has been described by a former Bishop of Chester as very early Anglo-Norman.

During the centuries the fabric of the church suffered and when it was restored in 1772, it was re-dedicated to St Helen; the apse - a circular addition at the East end - was changed to an oblong, and the windows were replaced.

OVERTON CHURCH.

St Helen's Church, Overton
(A drawing made about 1898)

There were box pews which were removed when the chancel was refurbished in 1902, and all the old high pews were replaced at the same time.

The pulpit was originally a three decker, the lower portions being removed in 1902.

There were musicians in the gallery during the first half of the 19th century. There are accounts for the purchase of a bassoon, clarinet and oboe in 1814, and later a violoncello.

Lancaster Priory appropriated the chancel in 1246. A separate parish was formed in 1765.

According to the records it has been revealed that Overton had a shipyard which was in existence before 1670 when it was sold for the sum of £10. In 1746 it was sold again to Mr Thomas Woodhouse for £31.10s. The business remained in the hands of this family at least until 1948.

The Old Signal Cannon ...

- a warning cannon to warn shipping off dangerous rocks off Overton - disappeared in a storm about 1908. A Russian ship went down in this storm. The cannon has never been found. Is it still in deep water?

Recollections of Overton and Sunderland Point (*Jean Exton*)

... And the tide came in

The year would be 1932 or 33. The afternoon was beautifully warm and sunny when I, accompanied by my parents after an afternoon at The Point, began to make our way back on foot, to Overton along the narrow tidal road when suddenly, swirling water appeared over the road. At about the same moment, a motor vehicle drew up alongside, also intending to return to Overton. The water was coming in very fast and the driver realised that as the road dips in places and has many twists and turns, he would be unable to ascertain the route, and no doubt remembering the quite steep channels in some places. He had come too far to reverse back to The Point and I now realise the road would have been too narrow to turn his motor car round. The driver invited my parents to climb up onto the roof of his vehicle and remain there with him and his passenger, until the water receded. I can remember being lifted up and being spellbound as the water rose higher and higher completely surrounding his vehicle. The whole incident is as clear as if it occurred yesterday and each time I pass the spot, I remember what happened so long ago when I would have been 5 or 6 years of age.

My father 'Bert' Holmes and like myself, Heysham born and bred, knew the whole area well - Heysham, Middleton, Overton, Sunderland Point etc, the latter being a particular favourite for him and to where he would *walk* the family on summer

Overton

Sundays from our home in Maple Avenue, Sandylands. We made the journey on numerous occasions, either just by ourselves or with friends or any visiting family, but this was the only occasion father apparently miscalculated the tide's arrival.

My father was quite well known in this area mainly due to working for over 40 years for J Snowden & Co, house furnishers of Morecambe. His father, my granddad 'Rowley' Holmes, owned two butchers shops in the West End of Morecambe and was contracted to supply the workforce engaged in the construction of Heysham Harbour, with fresh meat which he delivered by hand-cart twice weekly, accompanied by my father who would have been 6 or 7 at the time.

This quaint mode of transport for the conveyance of fresh meat and at considerable distance, come rain or shine, seems quite comical, albeit arduous too!

Heysham Peninsula
17. *Middleton*

The Old Roof Tree Inn
Historic Listed Building

(The text below is copied from the Inn by courtesy of the landlord.)

The inn has a fascinating history dating back more than 650 years.

Before the first building was erected, the whole village of Middleton was owned by Sir Edward de Nevill who gave half of his land to Cockersand Abbey in 1337 on condition that an 'honest secular priest' be provided to sing daily for the souls of the dead in Middleton Chapel. Nine years later, the Abbot of Cockersand was recorded as paying 7d for his land in Middleton and the monks had built a farm on the site of the present Old Roof Tree Inn. (The Buttery used by the monks is, today, a dining area of the inn.)

The unusual name 'Roof Tree' originates from the technique used in its construction.

The monks used whole trees to make up the timber frame of the structure in a similar fashion to the A-frame of a modern day tent. A whole tree trunk would be used as a ridge pole or 'Roof Tree' running across the top of the structure to provide stability.

Henry VIII carried out the dissolution of the monasteries including Cockersand Abbey and the building became possessed by the Crown. Later in history the building was very much a part of the English Civil War. In the 1640s it was owned by the Middleton family who were supporters of the Royalist cause during the Civil War. The family had all its lands, including the Roof Tree building, sequestrated by Oliver Cromwell's forces.

The property was bought by William West, a colonel in the Roundhead army and member of Cromwell's Parliament. Indeed, an original letter from Oliver Cromwell summoning him to Parliament has been framed and hangs in the inn to this day.

Recollection of aircraft on Middleton Sands

One of the aircraft on Middleton Sands was owned by my uncle, Jim Procter (opticians in Preston). He used it for excursions etc. I was only a little girl at the time. That was in the late 1930s. He was in the Air Force during the war.

Heysham Peninsula
18. Sunderland Point

(For greater detail on Sunderland Point see the detailed account by Hugh Cunliffe[1].)

Perhaps the most picturesque way to reach Sunderland Point is from Lancaster via the Golden Ball referred to nowadays as 'Snatchems'. The Inn was notorious for the press gangs, which were known for their kidnapping of men to crew the local ships. Perhaps some of them were needed for the ships at Sunderland Point.

It was also a centre for the slave trade, shipping slaves up the river to Lancaster.

Golden Ball Inn, Snatchems

The tide washes twice a day through the channels on the road to the Point, so it pays to take care and watch the tides. The settlement can be cut off for hours at the periods of spring (highest) tides, and the tide comes in fast.

Sunderland Point was a great area for shipping in its heyday. Ships were built at Overton and there was a great deal of trade between the Point and West Virginia. Apart from tobacco, rum and sugar, there were also unusual woods, mahogany etc. The company of Waring and Gillow made fine furniture from the wood and it was exported back to America.

At its peak Sunderland Point was said to rival Bristol as a port, and it was only when Glasson Dock was opened in 1787 that the north side of the river fell into decline.

It is a great place for painters; there are some very attractive houses and boats. On warm afternoons there is usually an artist with his easel, sometimes inviting visitors to watch.

There are always the wildfowl and gulls, and the wading birds which wait for the tide. At certain times of the year there are rarities to be seen.

Sunderland Point

Sunderland Point in 1908, Second Terrace, with Cotton Tree (Black Poplar)
Sketch by Rod Hargreaves (1999) from the original painting 'A Lancashire Village'
by William Page Atkinson Wells (1872-1923)

Sambo's Grave

One cannot leave Sunderland Point without visiting Sambo's Grave close to the Middleton shore, which is recorded as the last resting place of a negro slave who died soon after his arrival from the West Indies. His story is told in the memorial over his grave, dated 1796:

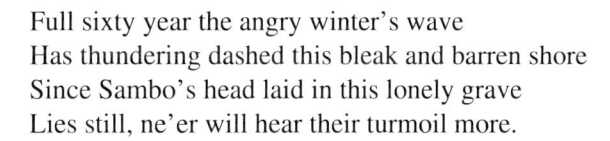

Full sixty year the angry winter's wave
Has thundering dashed this bleak and barren shore
Since Sambo's head laid in this lonely grave
Lies still, ne'er will hear their turmoil more.

Full many a sand-bird chirps upon the sod,
Any many a moonlight elfin round him trips;
Full many a summer's sunbeam warms the clod,
And many a teeming cloud upon him drips;

But still he sleeps, till the awakening sounds
Of the archangel's Trumpet new life impart;
Then the great Judge his approbation founds
Not on man's colour, but his worth of heart.

Reference

1. Hugh Cunliffe : *The Story of Sunderland Point* : pub. by author 1984 (New edition 1999). Printed by Trelawney Press Ltd, Morecambe

Bibliography

Arthur Casson et al : *History of Heysham* : unpublished c.1965

J C Procter : *St Patrick's Chapel* : Heysham Heritage Association 1997

T W Potter and R DAndrews : *Excavation and Survey at St Patrick's Chapel and St Peter's Church, Heysham, 1977-78* : Antiquaries Journal Vol LXXIV 1994

Edith Holden (ed.) : *The Country Diary of an Edwardian Lady* : Michael Joseph 1977

Graham Harvey : *The Killing of the Countryside* : Jonathan Cape 1997

Richard Mabey : *Flora Britannica* : Sinclair-Stevenson 1996

L A & P D Livermore : *The Flowering Plants and Ferns of North Lancashire* : pub. by authors 1987

Hugh Cunliffe : *The Story of Sunderland Point* : pub. by author 1984 (New edition 1999) Printed by Trelawney Press Ltd, Morecambe

Mary Levine : *Sunderland Point, Morecambe* : Lancashire Magazine, November/December 1987

Scrapbook article on *Sunderland Point* : Morecambe Guardian 23/8/1963.

Morecambe Lancashire Magazine : *Curious Lancashire* : January February 1988

Michael Bockmuhl : *J M W Turner, 1775-1851 The World of Light & Colour* : Benedikt Tashen 1993

A J Finberg : *The Life of J M W Turner RA* : Oxford University Press (2nd Ed.) 1961

David Hay : *In Turner's Footsteps, Through the Hills & Dales of Northern England* : John Murray 1984

T Dunham Whitaker : *A History of Richmondshire, Vol 2* : Longmans 1823

Farrer & Brownbill (eds) : *Victoria History of the County of Lancaster, Vol 8* : University of London, Institute of Historical Research 1914, rev. 1966

Morecambe Library : *Trade Directories* : 1824-5 and 1900

Morecambe Visitor : *Newspapers 1898 - 1904* and later on microfilm at Morecambe Library

Morecambe Gazette : 1900 Jan - Sept (*shortlived newspaper*)

National School, Heysham (now St. Peter's) : *Log Book* : c.1856 onwards

National School, Heysham : *Admission Register* : 1896 - c.1950

Public Records Office, Chancery Lane : *Rolls referring to Heysham*

Personal oral history collection (*audio tapes*)

Photographs courtesy of City and Maritime Museums, Lancaster.

Heysham Peninsula
Index

A
Angles	4
Anglo-Saxon	3-4, 17-19, 52
Archaeology	2-3, 14, 16, 18
Athelfrith	4

B
Bailey Lane	47
Baldwin Bent	27
Barrows field	2-3, 5,10
Battery	1, 32, 49
Baulk	3, 22, 36, 38
Bay Cottage	62
Bazil Point	11
Black Poplar	11-12, 71
Board School	53, 59-60
Bobbin Mill	35, 48
British Energy	8
Bushell, Mr (Rector)	20-21

C
Carr Garth	47-48
Casson, Arthur	3-4, 72
Casson, Frank	26
Celts	3-4, 16
Christianity	4
Clarkson, Rev Thomas	18, 53
Clarkson family	20, 50
Cockersand Abbey	18, 69
Colloway Marsh	5
Common Agricultural Policy	7
Cotton Tree (see Black Poplar)	
Cross Cop	1, 24

D
Danes	4
Dawson City	25, 29-32, 56-57, 59
de Moleyns, Stephen	47
Domesday book	4, 66
Druids	3
Dukes (of Lancaster etc)	33

E
English Nature	7
European Bison	26

F
Far Naze	1, 8
Fishing	3, 10, 36-38
Flints	2

G
Geology	1-3
Glasson Dock	70
Glebe Garden	19
Golden Ball (see Snatchems)	
Greese Cottage	20, 50

H
Half Moon Bay	1, 5, 8, 10
Halton	4
Heysham and Cumberland Mountains	20, 22
Heysham Banks	9, 25
Heysham Brass Band	28, 42
Heysham Golf Club	34, 56
Heysham Hall	54
Heysham Harbour	1-2, 5, 8-10, 25-27, 29-31, 33-35, 37, 59-61, 65, 68
Heysham Head	1, 10, 43-46
Heysham Lake	2, 8, 32
Heysham Moss	2, 11, 36
Heysham Tower	39, 41, 48, 54-55
Heysham Village	5, 10, 16, 20, 22-23, 27, 42, 44-45, 48, 51, 63-64, 66
Higher Heysham	28, 47
History of Richmondshire	21-22, 72
Hogarth, Dr Bertram	29,31
Hogarth, Dr Whewell	14, 29
Hogback stone	4, 18

I
Ice Age	2
Institute	63-65
Ireland	4, 13-14
Irish Sea	2, 10
Isle of Man	4, 33, 32

K
Klondyke	25-26, 28-29, 31, 33, 27, 56-60
Knowlys, John (Heysham Tower)	48
Knowlys Road	20

L
Lancashire Wildlife Trust	8, 11
Lancaster Priory	4, 47, 67
Long Barrow	2

Lord of the Manor	4	Royds family	18, 49-50, 55, 56, 64
Lune	2, 5, 11, 21, 37	Royds, Canon C C T	24
		Royds, Rev C T	24, 28, 31, 38, 55, 58, 63
		Royds, Rev J	17-18, 49, 56, 62,64

M

Main Street	20, 50
Manor House	4, 45
Middleton	2, 5, 8, 11-12, 37, 42, 67, 69, 71
Middleton Industrial Site	8, 12, 37
Middleton Sands	2, 11, 69, 71
Midland Railway Company	30
Mitchell, William (brewer)	28
Moneyclose Lane	9
Monsignor Gradwell	14
Morecambe & District Gazette	27, 31, 33, 72
Morecambe Bay	1-2, 9-10, 14, 22
Morecambe Visitor	25, 27, 59-61, 72
Mussels	3, 32, 38

Royal Society for the Protection of Birds 7-8, 12
Ruskin, John 22-23

S

Salem Farm	22
Sambo's Grave	71
Sandylands	31, 60, 68
Saxons	4
Shrimping	34-35, 37
Signal Cannon	67
Skears	1-3, 10, 13-14, 38
Snatchems	11, 70
Stephenson, William (gardener)	39-41
St Patrick	13-14, 66
St Patrick's Chapel	3, 5, 13-15,16, 72
St Peter's Church	10, 15, 16-19, 34, 72
St Peter's School	48, 53-60, 63
Stone Age	2
Stuttard, Arthur	34, 54-60, 63
Sunderland Point	5, 11, 37, 67, 70-72
Sunshine Slopes	1-2

N

National School	23, 28, 53-60, 63, 72
National Trust	5, 7
Nature Reserve	8-9, 12
Navvies	25-28, 30, 56-57, 59
Near Naze	1, 8, 26
Norse	3, 48

O

Old Hall, Heysham	49-50
Overton	2, 5, 11-12, 37, 42, 56, 66-67, 70

T

Teanel (tinnel)	3, 34
Throbshaw Point	1
Tostig	4
Tudors	52
Turner, J M W	20-23, 72

P

Picts	4
Pinky and Perky	43
Pot House	61, 62
Power Stations	1, 8-9

W

Waring and Gillow	70
Water Mill	47-48
Whitaker, Rev T D	18, 20-22, 50, 72
Wildlife	5-12
Wildlife Trusts	7
William the Conqueror	4
Woodhouse, William	23-24
Woodland Trust	7
World War I	48, 64
World War II	36, 65

R

Red Nab	1, 9, 26, 34
Rock-hewn graves	13
Romans	16, 51, 66
Roof Tree Inn, Middleton	37, 69
Rose Garden, Heysham Head	45-46
Royal Hotel	20-21, 42